AIRCRAFT OF
THE ACES

131 SPITFIRE ACES OF THE
CHANNEL FRONT 1941-43

SERIES EDITOR TONY HOLMES

131 AIRCRAFT OF THE ACES

Andrew Thomas

SPITFIRE ACES OF THE CHANNEL FRONT 1941-43

OSPREY
PUBLISHING

First published in Great Britain in 2016 by Osprey Publishing
PO Box 883, Oxford, OX1 9PL, UK
1385 Broadway, 5th Floor, New York, NY 10018, USA

E-mail: info@ospreypublishing.com

Osprey Publishing, part of Bloomsbury Publishing Plc

© 2016 Osprey Publishing Limited

All rights reserved. Apart from any fair dealing for the purpose of private study, research, criticism or review, as permitted under the Copyright, Design and Patents Act 1988, no part of this publication may be reproduced, stored in a retrieval system, or transmitted in any form or by any means, electronic, electrical, chemical, mechanical, optical, photocopying, recording or otherwise without prior written permission. All enquiries should be addressed to the publisher.

A CIP catalogue record for this book is available from the British Library

ISBN: 978 1 4728 1258 2
PDF e-book ISBN: 978 1 4728 1259 9
e-Pub ISBN: 978 1 4728 1260 5

Edited by Tony Holmes
Cover Artwork by Mark Postlethwaite
Aircraft Profiles by Chris Thomas
Index by Zoe Ross
Originated by PDQ Digital Media Solutions, UK
Printed in China through World Print Ltd.

16 17 18 19 20   10 9 8 7 6 5 4 3 2 1

Osprey Publishing supports the Woodland Trust, the UK's leading woodland conservation charity. Between 2014 and 2018 our donations will be spent on their Centenary Woods project in the UK.

www.ospreypublishing.com

Acknowledgements
The author wishes to thank the following pilots who have given of their time in presenting accounts or information for inclusion within this volume – Flt Lt Clive Anderton DFM, the late Wg Cdr J C Freeborn DFC, Air Vice-Marshal W H Harbison CB CBE AFC, the late Wg Cdr P L Parrott DFC, the late Flt Lt W B Peglar DFC, the late F J Twitchett and the late Air Commodore E W Wootten CBE DFC and bar AFC.

Front Cover
On 12 December 1942, the USAAF's Eighth Air Force undertook Mission No 25, when 90 B-17s were despatched to bomb two targets in France – 78 aircraft targeted the railway marshalling yards at Rouen, although due to cloud only 17 bombed. Twelve more mounted a diversion against Abbeville/Drucat airfield, where again the target was obscured and the aircraft returned without bombing.
   Part of the escort to cover the B-17s' withdrawal was provided by Spitfire VIs of No 124 Sqn, led by Sqn Ldr Tommy Balmforth. He led his unit in a climb to 28,000 ft so as to be at the correct altitude to meet the Flying Fortresses as they flew home. At around 1400 hrs, in good weather, over the mid-Channel between Dieppe and Beachy Head, the bombers were attacked by Fw 190s of II./JG 26. Balmforth's Spitfires swiftly intercepted the enemy aeroplanes and a series of dogfights ensued. Amongst the pilots involved was 20-year-old Londoner Flt Lt 'Slim' Kilburn, who was flying BR-579/OH-H. Reaching acedom during the course of the action, he described this event in his post-flight report;
   'I was "Yellow 1" when the squadron engaged ten-plus FW 190s that were preparing to attack the Fortresses on their return journey. I fired a four-second burst from 350 yards dead astern at one of the last FW 190s and it caught fire. I broke away and turned right round in time to see the enemy aircraft still on fire dive straight into the sea.
   'I later engaged another FW 190 that was on the tail of a Spitfire IX. I fired several short bursts with varying deflection in a quarter attack at 300 yards and then broke as there were other enemy aircraft about. My No 2 [future ace Sgt John Saphir] saw both the '190 and the Spitfire crash in the sea very close together. I took a camera gun film of both aircraft going down and crashing.'
   With three and one shared victories in the Spitfire VI, Kilburn was the most successful pilot on this mark (*Cover artwork by Mark Postlethwaite*)

Title Page
Channel Front ace Sqn Ldr 'Dickie' Milne, CO of No 222 Sqn, flies Spitfire VB AD233/ZD-F in April 1942 (*No 222 Sqn Records*)

Back Cover (top)
Pilots of No 453 Sqn RAAF brief at Southend for yet another sortie over the Channel during the summer of 1943 (*RAAF*)

CONTENTS

CHAPTER ONE
DEFENCE TO OFFENCE — 6

CHAPTER TWO
LEANING INTO EUROPE — 12

CHAPTER THREE
GREATEST AIR BATTLES — 48

CHAPTER FOUR
THE ENDLESS OFFENSIVE — 68

CHAPTER FIVE
PREPARING FOR INVASION — 83

APPENDICES — 88

COLOUR PLATES COMMENTARY — 90
BIBLIOGRAPHY — 95
INDEX — 96

CHAPTER ONE

DEFENCE TO OFFENCE

'I observed an ME 110 flying north east. The enemy aircraft attempted to escape by turning round and diving towards France. The enemy aircraft was at about 6000 ft, and made for a thin layer of cloud. I followed and delivered a quarter attack, opening fire at about 300 yards and closing to 25 yards, giving a four-second burst. The rear gunner was killed in my first attack, but had first fired two ineffective bursts. The enemy aircraft tried to escape by making several steep right- and lefthand turns. I then made a beam attack, followed by two attacks from astern. I observed the enemy aircraft catch fire, large pieces broke off and it dived into the sea. I then returned to base. I saw no attempt to bail out.'

Thus, shortly before 1000 hrs on 4 January 1941 off Selsey Bill, at the controls of Spitfire I X4478, Flg Off Brendan 'Paddy' Finucane of Tangmere-based No 65 Sqn claimed the type's first victory of the year. The 20-year-old Irishman's third victim was, in fact, probably Oberleutnant Rücker's Do 17Z 'U5+JK' of I./KG 2. By the time of his death 18 months later, Finucane had become a leading exponent of Supermarine's graceful fighter during the RAF's new offensive posture.

Having previously implemented a wholly defensive strategy in the face of the Luftwaffe's onslaught against Britain, the RAF, by the close of 1940, had countered the enemy's daylight bomber threat to such an extent that Fighter Command had begun to tentatively switch from defensive to offensive operations. The very first offensive operation mounted by Fighter

Victors and vanquished! Four pilots of No 92 Sqn survey the wreckage of Ju 87 Stuka 'J9+BK' of 2./StG 1 that they had just shot down over Manston on 5 February 1941. They are, from left to right, Plt Off Cecil Saunders, Sgt Ream, Sgt Hugh Bowen-Morris and Plt Off Ronnie Fokes. The share took Saunders to acedom, whilst for Fokes it was the penultimate of his 13 victories (*HMP via Martin Mace*)

Command had been undertaken on 20 December when a pair of Spitfires led by Flt Lt Pat Christie of No 66 Sqn strafed Le Touquet airfield. This was the first time Spitfires had operated over France since the French surrender.

As the new year dawned it was to witness a marked change in operational emphasis, Fighter Command slowly adopting an offensive posture that saw it taking the fight to the enemy. Initially, small numbers of Spitfires and Hurricanes flew into France, but soon larger operations that saw fighters escorting bombers (the latter being involved in part to draw the Luftwaffe up into battle) were being routinely flown. Thus, Pat Christie, a six-victory ace, had paved the way for countless offensive sorties by the RAF over the next three years. The operational codenames of 'Circus', 'Ramrod', 'Rodeo', 'Rhubarb', 'Ranger' and others quickly became achingly familiar to RAF fighter pilots.

A 'Rhubarb' was an offensive sortie by a small section of fighters, usually pairs, to attack targets of opportunity such as trains, or fixed targets. 'Circus' denoted an attack by bombers heavily escorted by fighters, the presence of the former being to entice enemy fighters into combat, whilst on a 'Ramrod' bombers, again heavily escorted by fighters, had the primary task of destroying a target. In contrast, a 'Ranger' was a sweep in which a large formation of fighters flew a freelance intrusion over enemy territory with the express aim of destroying enemy fighters.

The new offensive policy would generally be implemented by units flying from bases in central and southern England assigned to Nos 10, 11 and 12 Groups. On 1 January 1941 Fighter Command fielded 15 Spitfire squadrons split between No 11 Group in southern England, No 12 Group in the Midlands and No 10 Group in the west, although these were easily reinforced when required.

The first victory claimed by Fighter Command in 1941 fell to Flg Off 'Paddy' Finucane of No 65 Sqn on 4 January. The Bf 110 he downed was his third confirmed success. By the summer of 1942 the diminutive Irishman had become the leading ace over the Channel Front (via Chaz Bowyer)

Initially, however, the year started with defensive activity. Four hours after 'Paddy' Finucane opened the Spitfire account for 1941, 19-year-old ace Plt Off Eric 'Boy' Marrs of Warmwell-based No 152 Sqn claimed his penultimate victory when he shared in the destruction of a Do 17Z from *Wekusta* 26, flown by Gefreiter Werner Seurig, with anti-aircraft guns. Marrs wrote in his diary;

'I saw an aeroplane about three miles northeast of me, about 2000 ft higher up, and going west-northwest. I opened up everything and aimed to cut it off. It looked very slim and had two rudders, and I thought it might have been a Hampden, although I was pretty sure it was a Dornier. I soon came close enough to see a large black cross on its side and recognised it as a Dornier 17. I approached from the sea and opened fire at about 400 yards from the port rear quarter. He then turned south and dived like stink for the clouds. I turned in behind him and, closing to about 250 yards, fired at the fuselage and two engines in turn. Black and white smoke came from the engines and all return fire from the gunners ceased. I was overshooting, and just before he reached the clouds I had to break away. I was therefore overjoyed to hear that he had come down in the sea, and that boats had gone out to look for survivors. Nobody was found. Needless to say, there was rejoicing in Bournemouth last night. I must say I have been phenomenally lucky with these lone aircraft.'

Not all intercepts ended as well as this one did, as Flt Lt Billy Drake later recalled;

'On 7 January 1941 I had two encounters when on patrols off Dover. With "Orange" O'Meara, we jointly damaged a Ju 88, and then on a later sortie I inflicted some damage on another of them off Folkestone. A few days later No 421 Flight was expanded to become No 91 Sqn. I was given command of "A" Flight under the excellent Paddy Green, who became a squadron leader.'

'RHUBARBS', 'CIRCUSES' AND 'RAMRODS'

After a period of dreadful weather, the first manifestation of the new offensive policy came during the cold, clear morning of 10 January 1941 when the first 'Circus' operation, aimed at drawing Luftwaffe fighters into combat, was flown. It was a modest effort consisting of just six Blenheims from No 114 Sqn, escorted by a dozen squadrons of fighters, targeting an ammunition dump near Calais. The Spitfires of Nos 41, 64, and 611 Sqns provided the top cover while those of Nos 66, 74 and 92 Sqns undertook rear cover and No 610 Sqn was part of the target support.

Over the coast the Blenheims encountered heavy flak, whilst the fighters were engaged by Bf 109s from I. and II./JG 3. As well as the loss of a Hurricane, several Spitfires were hit, one of which was P7561 of No 74 Sqn that Sgt Laurence Freese crashed on landing. He later succumbed to his injuries, the first Spitfire pilot to die on the new offensive operations. In return, after being jumped by five Bf 109s, Sgt Aubrey Baker of No 41 Sqn in P7816 probably destroyed an enemy fighter. His seventh claim would be the first of many made by Spitfire pilots participating in the new offensive.

Fighter Command's prime purpose was of course defending Britain, as the Luftwaffe continued to make daylight incursions well into 1941. Under the cover of foul weather, during a convoy escort off the Lincolnshire coast on the afternoon of 15 January, Flg Off 'Cocky' Dundas and Plt Off 'Johnnie' Johnson of No 616 Sqn found a 'bandit', as the latter described;

'It was a perfect interception. We were up-sun and higher than the Do 17. But he saw us when we streaked down, and whirled round for Holland in a fast diving turn.'

Nonetheless, the pair attacked and saw the undercarriage drop before the bomber limped off with the port engine smoking. The Do 17 was probably the aircraft from II./KG 3 that crash landed at Antwerp. Although the pair could only claim it damaged, the aeroplane was, nevertheless, the first combat claim for Johnson, who was to end the war as the most successful Spitfire pilot of them all with 41 victories – 27 of them on offensive operations from England. Four days after this, another future Spitfire icon was successful, again during a defensive sortie, when No 65 Sqn's 'Paddy' Finucane shot down a Ju 88 in concert with Sgt Harold Orchard, the Irishman writing

One of the units that was heavily involved in the early cross-Channel operations from Manston and Biggin Hill was No 92 Sqn. Amongst the fighters it flew on these sorties over the Continent was R6923/QJ-S, which was built as a rare cannon-armed Mk IB and delivered to No 19 Sqn in July 1940. The fighter was relegated to No 7 OTU when persistent jamming with its two 20 mm weapons saw all Mk IBs swapped by No 19 Sqn for standard Spitfire IIAs. Converted into a Spitfire VB in April 1941, the aeroplane was then issued to No 92 Sqn. It was regularly flown by ace Flg Off Alan Wright, who made several claims in the aircraft prior to it being shot down by Bf 109s (possibly from JG 26) over the Channel on 21 June 1941 during 'Circus 16'. R6923's pilot, Sgt G W Ashton, bailed out and was rescued (*P H T Green collection*)

that, 'When last seen, both engines were aflame and the enemy aircraft was losing speed rapidly, about five miles from the French coast'.

Luftwaffe reconnaissance operations also continued, with the Royal Navy's fleet anchorages in Scotland being routinely targeted. It was against one of these that Spitfires of the veteran No 603 Sqn, based at Drem, were scrambled on the afternoon of the 24th. Flg Off 'Ras' Berry (in P7564) and Flt Lt John Boulter (P7597), both aces, were among those sent aloft, and they spotted the intruder – a Ju 88 – climbing ten miles east of May Island. Only Sgt Strawson was able to fire a short burst, however, before it was lost in cloud.

Coincident with the switch to offensive operations was the gradual delivery to No 92 Sqn of Spitfires with greater 'punch'. Having received four cannon-armed Spitfire IBs during November 1940, the unit received a further four – R6904, R6919, R6923 and R6924 – at its Manston base on 22 January. No 92 Sqn had demonstrated their effectiveness on 1 December when the Bf 109 engaged by ace Flt Lt 'Pancho' Villa fell apart after it was hit by his cannon fire. It was in one of these aircraft (X4272/QJ-D) that Flg Off Tony Bartley opened the unit's account for 1941 when, on the morning of 3 February, he claimed his ninth victory over the Thames Estuary. He had shot down Leutnant Max Petry's He 111 Wk-Nr 5517 'A1+AN' of 6./KG 55 off Southend. The squadron also received some interim Mk Vs for use alongside the cannon-armed Mk IBs – effectively they were Mk Is fitted with Merlin 45 engines. On 6 March

1941 the hybrid Spitfire V was ordered into quantity production, initially as a temporary expedient, but it was to be the most widely used Spitfire variant over the Channel Front during the mid-war years, with 6479 being produced.

Gradually, too, through the year more units were newly formed or were re-equipped with the Spitfire. One was No 145 Sqn under the command of Battle of Britain ace Sqn Ldr William Leather. Amongst his pilots was future ace Sgt Bill Johnson, who noted;

'Re-equipped with Spitfires from January 1941. Spitfire IIs were not available until late February when the squadron again became operational. During this short re-equipment the squadron remained at Tangmere, where we stayed, or at Merston, the satellite, as part of the Tangmere Wing, soon to be led by D R S Bader.'

As the weather improved high-level fighter sweeps and bomber escorts began, and the Luftwaffe was soon rising to the challenge. 'Circus No 2' was mounted against coastal airfields on the afternoon of 2 February, and among the escorts were Spitfires from six squadrons. Arriving over the target area at 19,000 ft at 1400 hrs, Spitfires from Biggin Hill (Nos 66, 74 and 92 Sqns) spotted six Bf 109s from 1./JG 3 below them. No 74 Sqn's CO, high-scoring ace Sqn Ldr 'Sailor' Malan (flying P7542), led his men down. In a brief combat off Boulogne he and Sgt Payne each claimed one fighter shot down – probably those of Unteroffizier Müller and Unteroffizier Pöpel, the latter crashing near Boulogne wounded. These were the first confirmed victories of the new offensive over the Continent.

Three days later a quartet of No 92 Sqn fighters led by Battle of Britain ace Plt Off Ronnie Fokes (in Spitfire I X4614) left Manston at 0845 hrs for a convoy patrol off Ramsgate. After an hour they spotted an explosion on a trawler and then saw a Ju 87 Stuka, which was one of a *Kette* from 2./StG 1 flying one of the dive-bomber's last missions against targets on the Channel Front. Fokes led Flg Off Cecil Saunders in a head-on attack as Leutnant Ernst Schimmelpfennig desperately tried to avoid the Spitfires, each of which took turns in firing at the evading Ju 87 that gradually manoeuvred over land. Eventually, as it turned over Manston, Fokes got in a telling burst and 'J9+BK' Wk-Nr 5225 blew up and crashed, killing the pilot and his gunner Obergefreiter Hans Kaden. The victory was shared by all four pilots, and it took Cecil Saunders to acedom – the first Spitfire pilot to achieve this distinction during the year. It was witnessed by his CO, Sqn Ldr Johnny Kent;

'The Stuka reached the edge of the airfield almost directly above me at about a hundred feet. Here, he was headed off by one of the Spitfires, and I could clearly see both gunner and pilot in their cockpits with the de Wilde ammunition bursting around them. The Spitfire overshot and pulled away and the German made another desperate attempt to land and turned violently to port, but at this instant Plt Off Fokes, in my aeroplane, flashed past me and gave a short burst with the cannons. I can still hear the " thump-thump-thump" of them followed by the terrific "whoosh" as the Stuka blew up and crashed just outside the boundary of the airfield.'

This was proved to be the last Ju 87 to fall on British soil.

Later that afternoon (5 February) a 'Circus' was mounted by six Blenheims against St Omer airfield, the escort including five squadrons flying Spitfires. Between the target and the coast the Bf 109s of I./JG 3 intervened, and they were in turn engaged by No 611 Sqn. Plt Off Barrie Heath, a Cambridge science graduate flying X4817, achieved his second success, as was later described by future ace Plt Off Wilf Duncan-Smith, who was in Spitfire I X4253;

'It was clear and sunny. Suddenly four Me 109s dived passed us on the left and six more came in on our formation from the right. The 109 in front of me jerked right, bringing me into a good position for a quarter attack, and I gave him a couple of quick bursts. I saw de Wilde strikes on the wing root and a piece flew off – the '109 rolled on its back and dived vertically. I broke off and chased after Barrie, not wanting to lose him. Barrie fired another burst and his target '109 steepened its dive, smoke trailing. Then he pulled up and swung left in a wide arc. I continued to watch, fascinated. The '109 never wavered from its headlong plunge until I finally saw it disappear into a wood and explode.'

No 65 Sqn was also involved, and at the controls of Spitfire II P7694 Flg Off Paddy Finucane shot down a Bf 109 over the Pas de Calais near Alprecht to become the first Spitfire pilot to 'make ace' on cross-Channel operations. However, it was very much the enemy's day as seven RAF fighters were shot down, with five pilots being killed and two captured. One of the latter was Sgt Dave Denchfield of No 610 Sqn, who was the 40th victim of the *experte* Hauptmann Walter Oeseau. Ominously, 5 February also saw the return to Abbeville and Le Touquet of Oberstleutnant Werner Mölders with the leading elements of JG 51, newly equipped with the much improved Bf 109F.

These losses on 5 February were the precursor for three years of frenetic, and often bloody, aerial warfare over the Channel Front.

CHAPTER TWO

LEANING INTO EUROPE

During 9 February a formation of RAF fighters swept across the Channel at high level 'trailing their coats' to challenge the Germans into combat. It was the start of the new Fighter Command policy of 'leaning into France', although this particular mission proved to be uneventful. Indeed, the only action of the day came when a patrol of No 64 Sqn Spitfires shot down Unteroffizier Hans Weber and his crew in Ju 88A-5 Wk-Nr 8102 '4D+FH' of II./KG 30 over the Thames Estuary – a first step to acedom for Sgt Tom Savage, whilst it was a second victory for Sqn Ldr Jamie Rankin.

However, aces soon began falling too, with Flt Lt John Boulter of No 603 Sqn becoming the first to die in 1941 when he collided with a Hurricane on takeoff on 13 February. The following day Battle of Britain ace Flt Lt 'Dizzy' Allen of No 66 Sqn was on patrol when his fighter (P7504) was hit by a Bf 109, probably from II./JG 52, over southeast England. With his Spitfire badly damaged and his right arm hanging limply and spurting blood, he gamely manoeuvred onto his attacker's tail, only to find that his guns were inoperable! He managed to force land at Biggin Hill, where it was discovered that his aeroplane had been holed 43 times by enemy fire – Allen had the dubious distinction of being the first ace wounded in action in 1941. II./JG 52 had only returned to the Channel 24 hours earlier, and its pilots claimed four No 66 Sqn Spitfires destroyed on 14 February, one of which fell to the guns of Major Hanns Trübenbach.

The Spitfire IIs of Hornchurch-based No 54 Sqn were led by ace Sqn Ldr Robert Finlay Boyd during early offensive operations. Amongst the aircraft serving with the unit at this time was P7666/KL-Z, named *OBSERVER CORPS*. It was used by Plt Off Jack Stokoe to claim his seventh victory on 20 April when he shot down a Bf 110, although he was also forced to bail out himself when the Spitfire was hit by enemy fire (*P H T Green Collection*)

Technical failure also caused losses such as on the 21st when, on patrol over Ramsgate at 32,000 ft, Spitfire P7816/EB-G of No 41 Sqn, flown by Sgt John Gilders, was seen to peel off and dive away, its pilot probably having fallen victim to oxygen starvation. No trace of the ace was found until 1994, when the wreckage was discovered and the 21-year-old was buried with full military honours. It was another blow to No 41 Sqn, which had lost two pilots to the guns of Major Werner Mölders the previous day.

Small-scale 'Rhubarbs' increasingly featured on flying programmes, with three pairs of Spitfires from No 611 Sqn leaving Hornchurch at intervals under the cover of bad weather on 20 February. The experience of Red Section was fairly typical. One aircraft crossed the coast, strafing a boat near Gravelines, whilst the second pilot in the section, finding clear sky over Cap Gris Nez, spotted a yellow-nosed Bf 109 and engaged it over Wissant. He saw hits on the fighter before breaking off his attack and returning to base. Both pilots encountered heavy anti-aircraft fire, and over subsequent months this was to take a steady toll of aircraft undertaking similar sorties. And whilst most Bf 109s encountered were still E-models, the improved F was increasingly being seen.

It was future ace Wg Cdr Harry Broadhurst, the Hornchurch Station Commander, who led Nos 54, 64 and 611 Sqns as cover for a returning 'Circus' during the afternoon of 25 February. Broadhurst was leading No 611 Sqn at 20,000 ft when, over Dunkirk, he brought his section in behind six Bf 109s of 6./JG 51. Firing a short burst, he shot down the leading Messerschmitt to claim his first Spitfire victory. In the general mêlée Flt Lt Douglas 'Dirty' Watkins (flying P7607) attacked another when in a dive on the outside of the turn;

'I then followed him down in a vertical dive, firing short one-second bursts without effect – I held him quite easily in the dive. I pulled out of the dive in a lefthand turn and saw the enemy aircraft start pulling out at about 5000 ft. He hit the sea about 200 yards off the coast.'

In improving weather sweeps became more regular, and whilst RAF losses began to mount, so did successful claims. One was made at around 1620 hrs on 1 March when No 74 Sqn was engaged, New Zealander Plt Off Bob Spurdle (flying Spitfire IIA ZP-T) being credited with downing

In the combat on 1 March, when Flt Lt Mike Newling of No 145 Sqn claimed his last success (a Ju 88), the victory was also shared with Flg Off 'Nobby' Clarke and Sgt Frank Twitchett. The latter was flying P7986/SO-J (*F J Twitchett*)

a Bf 109 near Cap Gris Nez. As he approached Ramsgate on the way home he shot down a second Messerschmitt to become an ace. Sgt John Glendinning got a third Bf 109 for his fifth claim, although was in turn shot down by Major Werner Mölders on the 12th.

The evening of 1 March also saw No 145 Sqn's Flt Lt Mike Newling, who had received the DFC the previous month, elevated to acedom. Whilst on a defensive sortie in P7916/SO-B southwest of Selsey Bill, he was involved in the destruction of Ju 88A-5 Wk-Nr 5147 '3Z+DR' of III./KG 77, flown by Oberleutnant Walter Fick and crew. Newling shared No 145 Sqn's first Spitfire victory with Flg Off D H 'Nobby' Clarke (in SO-C) and Sgt Frank Twitchett (in SO-J). Four days later Plt Off Jack Stokoe of No 54 Sqn was on a sweep southwest of Boulogne in Spitfire II P7281/KL-O when he shot down a Bf 109 for his sixth victory. This was also his first success of the year.

WING LEADERS

Gradually the Spitfire units received better aircraft, with several replacing their Mk Is with Mk IIs, whilst some received cannon-armed Mk Vs. New units also continued to be formed, including No 485 Sqn, the first RNZAF fighter unit established in Britain and one that nurtured a succession of very successful aces and leaders. As well as performing daytime operations, through the early winter months some squadrons conducted night flying training, maintained readiness and flew sector patrols and convoy escorts. One such unit was Wittering-based No 266 Sqn under future ace Sqn Ldr 'Jamie' Jameson, one of just two RAF survivors of the sinking of the aircraft carrier HMS *Glorious* in June 1940 during the Norwegian campaign.

The unit often flew night patrols in spite of very unfavourable weather conditions, and these bore fruit on 8 March when Sgt John von Schaick scored No 266 Sqn's first success of 1941. Flying Spitfire I X4164, he shot down Ju 88A-5 Wk-Nr 0404 'F6+BM' flown by Oberfelwebel Beuker, the 4(F)./122 machine crashing off Skegness. However, von Schaick's wingman, Plt Off Freddie Ferris in X4594, was hit by return fire and lost.

'Fighter Night' sorties by Spitfires continued to be flown to help counter the night Blitz, and their pilots gained several successes in the coming weeks. One was Australian Flt Lt Des Sheen of No 72 Sqn, who, flying K4596 on the night of 13/14 March, shot down a Ju 88 over the sea north of Acklington to make him the first Spitfire pilot to achieve acedom with a night victory. Another aviator had joined this elite band two days earlier when a trio of No 234 Sqn Spitfires flown by Sqn Ldr Minden Blake, Flt Lt Edward Mortimer-Rose and Plt Off 'Bertie' Wootton caught a reconnaissance Bf 110 of 1(F)./123 off Portland Bill and shot it down. This success gave Blake his eighth victory, Wootten his third and made Mortimer-Rose an ace. That same day No 222 Sqn's South African-born ace Flt Lt Brian van Mentz (in P7697) shared in the destruction of a Do 17 off Sheringham with Plt Off Klee to claim his final victory.

The most significant development of the period, and one that was to influence the character of Fighter Command's offensive operations through the mid-war years and beyond, was the introduction of Wing Leaders.

During the spring of 1941 the first Wing Leaders were appointed. At Biggin Hill, Wg Cdr A G 'Sailor' Malan was promoted to the position. His 'Ten rules of air fighting' became an unofficial bible for Fighter Command (via N L R Franks)

Officially titled Wing Commander (Flying), these individuals were all highly experienced and, at least initially, predominantly aces. They would lead their Wings in the air on cross-Channel operations that were a logical development of the controversial 'Big Wing' idea from the Battle of Britain. The position of Wing Leader was introduced to allow better control of fighter squadrons in the air during large-scale operations. By early 1941 Wings already existed at all the main fighter airfields in Nos 11 and 12 Groups in southern England, most consisting of three squadrons. Eventually, all comprised Spitfire squadrons, although when the Wing Leader concept was introduced on 19 March only the following were equipped with the aircraft;

Biggin Hill Wing (Nos 74, 92 and 609 Sqns) – Wg Cdr 'Sailor' Malan (20 victories)
Hornchurch Wing (Nos 54, 64 and 611 Sqns) – Wg Cdr Andrew Farquhar (5 victories)
Tangmere Wing (Nos 145, 610 and 616 Sqns) – Wg Cdr Douglas Bader (14 victories)
Duxford Wing (No 19 Sqn) – Wg Cdr Michael Crossley (22 victories)

The Wings at North Weald, Northolt and Duxford's Nos 310 Sqn all flew Hurricanes, and in the future Wings were also formed at fighter stations further west under No 10 Group control. Additionally, the COs of all but one of the ten Spitfire squadrons was also an ace, or a future ace, and most of those that survived the coming months would themselves become Wing Leaders in England or in the Western Desert, where the concept was also adopted.

For defensive operations the Sector Controllers would launch an appropriate response that could range in size from a section of just two aircraft through to a whole squadron of 12 Spitfires. Indeed, the day the Wing Leaders formally came into being No 92 Sqn flew an 11-aircraft patrol at 36,000 ft over Hastings with its new Spitfire Vs, led by Sqn Ldr Jamie Rankin. During the course of the mission the propeller of the CO's aircraft (X4257) suffered a constant-speed unit (CSU) failure due to its oil freezing at extreme altitude. He and two other pilots who experienced a similar problem all had to force land. Thereafter, until modifications were forthcoming, the throttles had to be constantly worked to keep the oil moving in the CSU on the Mk V. The reliability of the Spitfire VB's drum-fed cannon armament also gave rise to concern, as No 92 Sqn's Sgt 'Johnnie' Johnson explained;

'With the Hispano it was not unknown for the extractor to fail and leave an empty case in the chamber. The HE [high-explosive] shells we used were pre-set of course, and if a new round was then fed into the chamber you had a situation where the shell could explode in your wing.'

CHAPTER TWO LEANING INTO EUROPE

Although still covering the defence of the Midlands and the east coast, No 266 Sqn flew its first offensive mission using a forward base on 23 March.

Despite the night Blitz still being at its height, the Luftwaffe continued to mount daylight incursions too. Plt Off Bob Spurdle of No 74 Sqn engaged enemy bombers performing such missions on two occasions off Ramsgate, although, as he recalled in his autobiography, the interceptions did not go according to plan;

'By this time I was a section leader, and with Sgt Dales had two exciting encounters. On 24 March we caught a Ju 88 and claimed a probable – the enemy aircraft just held us off, with its port engine stopped and smoke and glycol pouring out. We were out of ammo and were merely waiting for the Hun's end to claim it as destroyed. The flak batteries of Dunkirk gave us a pasting and drove us away from our victim. When '109s came out to interfere we didn't see its finish.'

In fact their victim, a Ju 88A-5 from 3(F)./11 flown by Oberfeldwebel Gerhard Lilienthal, crash landed on a beach at Calais with both of its engines knocked out. The pair was in action off Ramsgate again the next day;

'As I gave the "Tally Ho!" and bent forward to adjust the gunsight graticule, I realised to my horror that the silhouette I took to be an aeroplane turning away was, in fact, a Do 215 turning to face us! I just had time for a quick squirt. I saw some strikes, then pulled the stick back and, as my kite heaved up, the bomber roared between us, actually passing below me and above Sgt Dales. As it passed we were hit by bullets from its front gun – both of our aeroplanes had a bullet hole in the starboard wing! By the time we'd pulled ourselves together and turned, the cocky Hun had escaped in a cloud bank and we were left flying around with red faces.'

On 30 March Flt Lt Tony Lovell (in X4683/EB-N) and Plt Off Archie Winskill of No 41 Sqn's 'B' Flight scrambled from Catterick in the early afternoon in overcast conditions to patrol off the Tees, where an incoming 'plot' had been detected. It was Ju 88A '4U+GH' of 1(F)./123 flown by Leutnant Wolfgang Schlott and crew, who had been tasked with flying a reconnaissance mission to Manchester. Shortly before 1500 hrs the Spitfire pilots spotted the enemy's vapour trail, as Lovell described. 'Climbed flat out in a climbing turn and followed the trail, which hid us very effectively'. Closing in to 250 yards, the Spitfires opened fire and damaged the bomber before it dived away towards cloud cover. Emerging from cloud over Redcar, the pilots resumed their attacks as the bomber skimmed the rooftops of the town and eventually crashed on Barnaby Moor, exploding when it hit the ground – it was Lovell's 11th victory.

Flying Spitfire I X4683/EB-N of No 41 Sqn, seen here at its Catterick base on 30 March 1941, Flt Lt Tony Lovell achieved his ninth victory when he shot down a Ju 88 near Ouston. The following day he also damaged an He 111 in the same aeroplane (*Harry Moyle*)

Four pilots of No 41 Sqn are shown the vulnerabilities of the He 111. Flg Off Tony Lovell is second from the right and to his left is another ace, Plt Off E V 'Mitzi' Darling. The latter was one of six No 403 Sqn pilots downed by JG 26 on 2 June 1942 during a sweep over France, Darling being killed (*via Steve Brew*)

Action over northern France also continued, such as on 31 March when, over the sea off Cap Gris Nez, No 91 Sqn's Sgt Jackie Mann was attacked by a Bf 109F of IV./JG 51 flown by Leutnant von Saalfeld. As the latter dived after the Spitfire, he momentarily lost control and the Bf 109 crashed into the sea without a shot having been fired. The demise of von Saalfeld elevated Mann to acedom. However, on 4 April, following an interception patrol in P7783, a badly burned Mann force landed at Hawkinge after combat with a Bf 109 flown by none other than Oberstleutnant Adolf Galland of JG 26. Sgt Arthur Spears (the nephew of World War I ace James McCudden VC) bailed out wounded following the same aerial engagement. Bob Spurdle also had a close shave at this time when, flying ZP-M on a 'Rhubarb' to St Omer, his fighter was attacked from the rear by a Bf 110 that suddenly appeared out of thick cloud;

'Something hit behind my head and exploded by my left elbow. "Whack! Whack!" Horrible jerks wrenched "M's" straining body, the jars violent through the joystick. Amazed at being hit in such a tight turn, I eased the stick forward and rolled her back and up into the cloud as my vision cleared. I saw it – an Me 110 still firing. Then the cloud wrapped its mantle around me – safe.'

Spurdle headed northwest for home, ruefully surveying the severe damage;

'It was impossible to think clearly while cloud flying, so I decided to come out and find out where I was and beat it for home. "M" and I burst

Originally formed at Hawkinge for 'Jim Crow' patrols, No 91 Sqn was active over the Channel throughout 1941. It was when flying this Spitfire VB off Margate on 7 May that Flg Off 'Spud' Spurdle probably destroyed a Bf 109 (*author's collection*)

through to green fields and a sleek grey shadow sliding along below. Hell's bells, another '110! Just three or four flashes from the rear gunner before "M's" leaden hail smashed down, the de Wilde's bursting red and winkling over the squared wings. I held the gun button down and a crazy pattern of torn earth streamed along, around, behind and beneath the Hun. The '110 lifted, dipped and flew straight in to the deck.

'A wild exultation surged over me. Got him! Three black trails of churned earth trailed behind like a speedboat's wash as the engines and fuselage skidded over the flooded fields.'

At Wittering, No 266 Sqn, which now included an increasing number of Rhodesians, continued to fly 'Fighter Night' patrols. It soon found success, as the CO, Sqn Ldr 'Jamie' Jameson, recalled in a letter to the author;

'In early 1941, the German night blitzes on our cities were becoming intolerable, so it was decided to stack our day fighters individually at about 200-ft intervals over the target area to try to spot the bombers against the moon or against the fires that they had started with thousands of incendiary bombs. We had no airborne radar at this stage of the war. My pilots achieved a certain amount of success on these operations, and I had two HE 111s confirmed and was credited with one damaged. The following will give some idea of the type of operation that the pilots of No 266 Sqn were carrying out at this time.

'On 8/9 April, whilst on patrol over Coventry, I sighted a HE 111 with one of our Defiant nightfighters formating on it below. I turned to join in but sighted another Heinkel above me against the moon, so I shot it down instead near Banbury. This success came on the same night that [Joseph] Goebbels christened the phrase "Coventrated" [following a 230-bomber raid on Coventry]. The next night Flt Lt Armitage almost repeated the feat during a raid on Birmingham, but he could only claim a probable.'

Offensive sweep operations over northern France also began, one early mission for No 266 Sqn being undertaken on 15 April when it joined Nos 65 and 402 Sqns. The unit got a taste of what could happen on these sweeps when Adolf Galland, on his way to a birthday party for World War 1 ace Theo Osterkamp at Le Touquet with his Bf 109F laden with lobster and champagne, conducted a small diversion during which he engaged No 266 Sqn's Spitfires and forced three of them to crash land!

Two days later another Spitfire pilot destined to become an ace claimed his first victory. His flight commander, seasoned Battle of Britain ace Flt Lt Al Deere, said of Canadian Flg Off 'Jack' Charles, 'He was a likeable chap, but did keep pretty much to himself. He was a bit of a loner – his only interest, outside of flying, was for the fairer sex'. On 17 April, whilst flying Spitfire II P7756 on a convoy escort east of Manston, Charles was vectored towards an intruder, as he subsequently reported;

New Zealander Flg Off Bob 'Spud' Spurdle became an ace with No 74 Sqn in April 1941, before joining No 91 Sqn. He later served with the RNZAF and claimed two victories against the Japanese over the Solomon Islands whilst flying Kittyhawks with No 16 Sqn (*R A Spurdle*)

Spitfire I X4646/OU-S of No 266 Sqn sits at dispersal in the spring of 1941, when it was regularly flying 'Fighter Nights'. Plt Off Andrew Humphrey first flew the aeroplane when he was scrambled to patrol overhead Wittering on 2 February 1941 (*Peter Cooke*)

'I ascertained it to be a '110. He did not see me until I fired at him in a quarter cum astern attack. I opened fire at 300 yards, closing to 50 yards, and silenced the rear gunner before the Messerschmitt pulled vertically into the thin cloud. I throttled back and followed up with a line astern burst of two seconds above cloud at a range of 50 yards. Bits were coming off, black smoke was coming from the port engine and white smoke from the other. I followed it though cloud and watched it smash into the Channel.'

Jack Charles' first victory was also No 54 Sqn's 100th!

In contrast, the next day one of the newer units, No 118 Sqn, moved to Ibsley to start offensive operations. It was led by Battle of Britain ace Sqn Ldr Frank Howell, of whom one of his contemporaries said, 'A good confident pilot and a natural leader, capable of getting the best out of people without much effort. A traditional, real fighter type'. No 118 Sqn flew the Spitfire II, but within days the new Spitfire V had claimed its first confirmed victory.

Shortly after 0900 hrs on 24 April, Sqn Ldr Jamie Rankin of No 92 Sqn (in R7161/QJ-J) was flying near Rye with Flt Lt Brunier when he shot down Feldwebel Günter Struck's Bf 109E 'Black 6' of 2./JG 52. The last pilot from the *Jagdgeschwader* to be shot down over Britain, Struck became a PoW. The next day, further down the coast, Sqn Ldr H deC A 'Paddy' Woodhouse, a future Wing Leader attached to No 610 Sqn to gain operational experience, shot down a Ju 88 – possibly Wk-Nr 3333 '3Z+FT' of 9./KG 77 flown by Oberleutnant Hans-August Richter – two miles off Brighton for the first of his five victories. Another future ace opened his account on the 26th when Plt Off Neville Duke of No 92 Sqn (flying R6904/QJ-Y) had his first combat during a high-level sweep up the Channel at maximum altitude – he damaged a Bf 109. In the same action Plt Off Ronnie Fokes shot down Unteroffizier Werner Zimmer of 4./JG 53 for his final victory, taking his total to 13.

The dangers for the pilots of Fighter Command were not confined to operational flying, however, as that same day the 'Ferry Inn' pub near Coltishall was struck by a stray bomb that killed a number of pilots, including eight-victory ace Flt Lt Brian van Mentz of No 222 Sqn.

Through the spring other pilots rose to the pantheon of aces, including the Belgian Flg Off Jean Offenberg of No 145 Sqn. On 5 May just north of

Sitting at Tangmere in April 1941, Spitfire IIA P7753/QJ-X of No 616 Sqn was the aircraft routinely flown by Flg Off 'Buck' Casson. On 5 May he used it to damage a Ju 88, although P7753 was hit by return fire and Casson forced to bail out (*L H Casson via T R Allonby*)

Pointe de Barfleur, on the Cherbourg Peninsula, he attacked several He 60 biplane reconnaissance seaplanes of 1./*SeenotGruppe* and shot one of them down and damaged a second. The following day Cambridge graduate Sqn Ldr Frederick 'Eric' Stapleton, flying as a supernumary with No 54 Sqn in order to gain experience prior to being given his own command, shot down a Bf 109 over the Channel to claim the first of his seven victories. However, within moments he was himself attacked by a Bf 109 flown by *experte* Major Frederick Beckh of IV./JG 51 and force to crash land his burning Spitfire near Dover. Stapleton was posted to command No 611 Sqn soon thereafter, before being promoted to become the Hornchurch Wing Leader in June. As he had discovered, the skies over southern England remained full of hazard.

Flg Off 'Buck' Casson of No 616 Sqn was hit and bailed out after combat with a Ju 88 near Tangmere on 5 May, and the following day No 616 Sqn's Flg Off 'Cocky' Dundas was hit and crash landed at Hawkinge – he had become the 68th victim of Oberstleutnant Werner Mölders, *Geschwaderkommodore* of JG 51. It was the *experte*'s final victory on the Channel Front. Ironically, Dundas was part of a section led by Wg Cdr Douglas Bader that was trialling the 'finger four' formation developed by Mölders during the Spanish Civil War and eventually adopted in Fighter Command.

Early the previous day (5 May), No 611 Sqn's Flg Off Tom Williams (in P7379) became an ace when, off Deal, he shot down a Bf 109. Squadronmate, and future ace, Sgt 'Mac' Gilmour (in P7503) claimed a second Messerschmitt for his first success. On 7 May fellow future ace Sgt Tommy Rigler of

The position of the Tangmere Wing Leader was given to the legendary legless pilot Wg Cdr Douglas Bader (*T R Allonby*)

To identify their aircraft Wing Leaders were permitted to use their initials in place of unit code letters. Malan's wore AGM, whilst Spitfire IIA P7966/DB was flown by Douglas Bader. His fighter also bore a rank pennant (*T R Allonby*)

No 609 Sqn opened his account when, between Dungeness and Calais, he shot down a Bf 109 in his very first aerial combat.

As the nocturnal Blitz approached its awful crescendo, on the night of 8/9 May No 266 Sqn at Wittering was ordered to fly some 'Fighter Night' patrols. One of the aircraft was flown by former Cranwell cadet Plt Off Andrew Humphrey, who, over Nottingham, attacked a He 111 of 6./KG 53 that came down near Grantham after four of the crew had bailed out. Two nights later the squadron enjoyed further success, as Sqn Ldr 'Jamie' Jameson described;

'I was on patrol at 14,000 ft over London. The city was one mass of flames and an enormous number of high-explosive bombs were dropping. It seemed that nobody could possibly survive in that holocaust below! My feelings were sadness for the people, anger against the Germans and frustration because I couldn't see the enemy aircraft that must have been all around me. Suddenly, I sighted a HE 111 at 10,000 ft against the light of the fires. I did a steep diving turn but lost sight of the Heinkel against a dark patch of ground. I continued to dive in the same direction and again picked it up, this time against the moon, and closed in to attack from astern and below.

'On opening fire at a range of 75 yards there was a big flash, and I could see my bullets hitting the enemy aircraft. Showers of sparks came from both engines and the aircraft suddenly lost speed and fell in a series of side to side glides, something like a falling leaf. I followed it down to 2000 ft but could not get in another burst as it was going so slowly. I lost it at this height against the dark ground, but it was confirmed later, having crashed at Chelmsford. I experienced intense return fire from the rear gunner and I could see tracer bullets flying past over my wing and beside the cockpit of my Spitfire.'

Flg Off Andrew Humphrey was also successful that night when, in an astonishing action, he claimed two Heinkels destroyed off the Dutch coast.

No 74 Sqn also flew some 'Fighter Night' patrols from West Malling. Taking off just before midnight on 10 May, Flg Off Roger Boulding

CHAPTER TWO LEANING INTO EUROPE

(in Spitfire II P8380/ZP-Q) was over London when he spotted He 111H 'A1+JN' of 5./KG 53 flown by Hauptmann Albert Hufenruther and shot it down at Kennington, near Ashford. Sadly, Boulding had little further opportunity to reach acedom as during a cross-Channel sweep in mid-June he had to bail out and was duly captured.

Although there had been considerable action on defensive operations through the spring, offensive 'Circus' and other missions had also continued in the improving weather. Increasingly, the Spitfires involved in these flights were improved Mk Vs. On 13 May, apparently without prior notice, eight new Spitfires VAs were delivered to No 611 Sqn. Several of the 'West Lancashire' unit's aircraft were financed locally, being named *City of Liverpool*, *City of Liverpool III* and *Fleetwood*. Their arrival coincided with that of Sqn Ldr Frederick Stapleton as CO. Sqn Ldr John Mungo-Park's No 74 Sqn also received its first Spitfire VB at this time, although it was in Spitfire II P8388/ZP-W on a 'Rhubarb' on 26 May that ace Flg Off Henry Baker shot down a Bf 109 over the Straits of Dover to claim his final victory.

No 603 Sqn had flown its first sweep led by Wg Cdr Andrew Farquhar a few days earlier when Nos 19 and 266 Sqns also headed down to West Malling for a 'Circus'. No 603 Sqn soon hit its stride, and its first big 'op' came on 28 May when it combined with Nos 54 and 611 Sqns in a sweep over Boulogne at high level. There, Flt Lt David Scott-Malden, a Cambridge classics graduate flying R7300/XT-R, re-opened No 603 Sqn's account when he probably destroyed a Bf 109.

It was further west, however, that the next ace over the Channel was spawned when, on the evening of 27 May, Cornish-based No 152 Sqn's Plt Off Graham Cox shot down a He 111 west of St Ives to achieve his fifth victory. Increasingly, however, it was on offensive operations that the Luftwaffe was met, as focus for the Germans had switched south and east for the invasion of the Balkans and, as yet unknown, the Soviet Union. Nevertheless, the skies remained hostile, and over the summer an increasing number of aces were lost, and others rested. June began with the loss, in No 54 Sqn Spitfire V R7275, of Battle of Britain ace Flt Lt George Gribble on a 'Roadstead'. He was shot down by a Bf 109 from

On 14 June 1941 Spitfires from the Hornchurch and Tangmere Wings escorted 12 Blenheim IVs on a 'Circus' to St Omer, during which No 92 Sqn's CO, Sqn Ldr Jamie Rankin, flying R7161/QJ-J, shot down the Bf 109E-7 flown by 18-victory *experte* Leutnant Robert Menge. His demise took Rankin to acedom (*P H T Green Collection*)

II./JG 53 and bailed out but was not found. On the same day, 4 June, Flt Lt Theo Buys, a former Netherlands East Indies Air Force pilot in No 611 Sqn, claimed the second of his four victories when he shot down a Bf 109. He reported;

'The enemy aircraft went spinning down, emitting black smoke and occasional jets of flame. I also saw a piece of his tail fly off. I followed him and saw him go into the sea about five miles off Folkestone.'

The following week, on the 14th, Spitfires from the Hornchurch and Tangmere Wings escorted 12 Blenheims on a 'Circus' to St Omer. During the course of the mission No 92 Sqn bounced 3./JG 26 as the latter climbed out from Audembert, resulting in 18-victory *experte* Leutnant Robert Menge being shot down and killed in Bf 109E-7 Wk-Nr 6490 by Sqn Ldr Jamie Rankin. Flying R7161/QJ-J at the time, Rankin achieved acedom with this success.

Two days later an attack on Boulogne Docks was opposed by more Bf 109s, which dived on No 92 Sqn. Flying high cover, No 74 Sqn's Spitfires went in pursuit of the enemy fighters. In the subsequent dogfight the unit's CO, Sqn Ldr John Mungo-Park, shot down a brace of Bf 109s. His first burst blew the entire tail assembly off a Bf 109, although he was then struck himself – at least one round hit the engine of his Spitfire. Mungo-Park was harried by a gaggle of Messerschmitts as he struggled home across the Channel, and when one overshot, having misjudged the slow speed of the Spitfire, the intrepid pilot fired the remains of his ammunition and it too went down. The crippled engine seized just off Folkestone and Mungo-Park was able to force land near Hawkinge. Three more Bf 109s fell during this mission, including one to No 92 Sqn's Plt Off 'Wimpey' Wade.

The action continued the next day when an attack on Choques by 23 Blenheims was supported by no fewer than 19 fighter squadrons, 13 of them flying Spitfires. A large-scale dogfight ensued, although the Hurricane units involved in the operation were more engaged. Nonetheless, No 92 Sqn's Sgt William Payne (in W3120) shot down a brace of Bf 109s between Boulogne and Le Touquet to become an ace in some style, as did No 609 Sqn's Flg Off Keith Ogilvie, whilst Plt Off John Bisdee claimed his sixth. A further 'Circus' was mounted on 18 June when Plt Off Wilf Duncan-Smith scored the first of his 19 victories, whilst 'Eric' Stapleton, now the Wing Leader, got his second, as Duncan-Smith vividly described;

'Off Gravelines we ran into two formations of eight Me 109s. 611 as bottom squadron had a perfect bounce, with 54 and 603 Sqns guarding from above. Eric's first attack produced a flamer which spiralled down into the sea. I got on the tail of one German and, closing on him from dead astern, opened

Sqn Ldr Jamie Rankin led No 92 Sqn with great success through the spring and summer of 1941, before becoming the Biggin Hill Wing Leader. He is probably sitting in Spitfire VB W3312, whose scoreboard shows ten of Rankin's eventual 22 victories (*author's collection*)

fire. To my satisfaction his tailplane disintegrated, bits flying everywhere, whereupon he did a most extraordinary upward corkscrew before spinning vertically down. I followed and watched with wonder as the enemy fighter broke up piece by piece.'

Ominously, however, Duncan-Smith noted, '"the Mark F" version [of the Bf 109] was making itself known more and more. This design had a lot more power and a slight edge on us for speed'.

21 June also proved to be a day of heavy fighting, and on a sweep led by 'Sailor' Malan, Flg Off Don Carlson of No 74 Sqn opened his account when he shot down a Bf 109 and Malan went one better with a brace of Messerschmitts destroyed. That day's 'Circus' was bounced from above by Bf 109Fs of JG 26, *Geschwaderkommodore* Oberstleutnant Adolf Galland shooting down one of the rear aircraft for his 70th victory. This success was almost his last, however, as he was then bounced by a Spitfire II from No 145 Sqn and the right side of his fuselage ripped open and his radiator and fuel tanks hit – the latter were seen to spew fuel. Galland was also hit by shell fragments. As he was gliding in to land his ruptured fuel tank finally blew up and he just managed to bail out of his disintegrating aircraft, Wk-Nr 6713. Galland's was a very significant scalp, and first step to acedom for Sgt Reg Grant.

Among the others engaged over the Pas de Calais was No 610 Sqn's newly arrived flight commander, Flt Lt Denis Crowley-Milling, who shared a Bf 109 to achieve his fifth victory. Also claiming his fifth that day was Gp Capt Harry Broadhurst near Calais, who, when leading the Hornchurch Wing, shot down two Bf 109s to reach ace status. No 54 Sqn's Flg Off Jack Charles enjoyed success too, using Spitfire VA R7279/KL-S *The Kings's Messenger* to claim his second victory. During the lunchtime 'Circus' No 603 Sqn was also in action, and later in the day future ace Flg Off Bill Douglas (flying W3110/XT-P) scored his first victory when he sent a Bf 109 down in flames off Cap Griz Nez. This was possibly Bf 109F-2 Wk-Nr 6732 of 8./JG 26, its pilot, Leutnant Heinz Greis, being killed.

As night fell all along Germany's eastern border, the Wehrmacht prepared for it latest offensive. A few hours later, as dawn broke, a massive offensive – codenamed Operation *Barbarossa* – opened against the Soviet Union. The war had now changed, and to give what support it could to the USSR, Churchill issued a directive that round-the-clock offensive air action should commence immediately. So began the 'Non-Stop Offensive' on the Channel Front.

NON-STOP OFFENSIVE

On the opening day of *Barbarossa* (22 June) a massive offensive was undertaken by Fighter Command squadrons that saw no fewer than 42 Bf 109s claimed destroyed. Although there was clearly a good deal of overclaiming on the 22nd, some pilots were indeed successful – including Biggin Hill's Wg Cdr 'Sailor' Malan, who downed a Bf 109 over Dunkirk.

Coltishall-based No 222 Sqn made its first offensive sweep over France that day (the unit usually flew escort to attacks on targets off the Dutch coast), and one of its pilots claimed a Bf 109F damaged. The 22nd proved hectic for those units sent across the Channel, No 611 Sqn's diarist describing the day's events 'as the best the Squadron had experienced since the previous September, when the Battle of Britain was at its height. At 1512 hrs the Squadron took off to rendezvous with 54 and 603 Sqns again, their task being high-level escort for another raid, this time on Hazebrouck railway yards, near the Belgian border.

'Ten Me 109s were seen climbing towards the Wing before the target was reached, and the Squadron went down to scare them before continuing on track. Above the target, the Wing split into fours, and large numbers of enemy fighters were encountered. At the end of the operation, 611 Sqn could make some significant claims, all involving Me 109s – Flt Lt Buys (one destroyed, one probable); Flt Lt Meares (one destroyed, one damaged); Plt Off Duncan-Smith (one destroyed); Flg Off Salmond (two destroyed); Sgt Gilmour (one destroyed, one damaged); Flg Off Pollard (one destroyed); Sgt Leigh (one probable); and Sgt Feely (one damaged). No Blenheims were lost.'

Dutchman Flt Lt Theo Buys recorded;

'We were at Gravelines at 18,000 ft when four ME 109Es approached us, turning to get behind. The section broke up and I attacked the leader of a pair, easily turning inside him, and got onto his tail. The enemy aircraft turned on his back and I was easily able to deliver a three-second burst, closing from 150 to 100 yards. The enemy aircraft dived vertically down emitting black and white smoke. I followed him down for 1000 ft and then circled, still watching him falling. When he was close to the ground my attention was diverted by three ME 109s 5000 ft above diving onto the section. I warned them over the R/T, broke away and returned towards Gravelines. I saw ahead of me two ME 109Fs 300 ft above, flying away from me. I closed in and attacked the rear enemy aircraft from astern and slightly below, opening fire at 30 yards' range with a two-second burst. The enemy aircraft exploded and flames shot out from the starboard side near the wing root. I watched him start to fall and returned home'

No 609 Sqn was also busy on the 22nd, engaging enemy fighters over the Calais-Gravelines area in the late afternoon. During this clash Flg Off John Bisdee (in W3115) and Plt Off Jean Offenberg (W3236) each shot down Bf 109s. However, the honours for the day went to squadronmate Sgt Tommy Rigler (in W3215, appropriately named *The Marksman*), who shot down three Messerschmitt fighters to become an ace with panache – he had only claimed his first victory on 8 May!

22 June was the start of a long summer for Fighter Command, with a significant rise in casualties following an increase in the distance the raids were penetrating into France, as Flt Sgt Don Kingaby of No 92 Sqn recalled;

'We were expecting a target about ten miles inside the coast, and it was some time before anyone believed that that was it – 50 miles in! We had no long-range tanks then, and 30 miles in meant a darned good flight and a landing at a forward base to refuel on the way home. What would it be like taking bombers in 50 miles?'

Next day, 23 June, future ace Plt Off Philip Archer shot down a Bf 109E southeast of Boulogne for his first success. Most squadrons experienced losses during this period, with No 611 Sqn's promising Theo Buys being posted missing on the 24th when he was shot down during a 'Circus'
he had claimed a Bf 109E for his fourth victory 24 hours earlier.

The following day came another significant loss during a Blenheim attack on Hazebrouck, as the Hornchurch Wing Leader, Battle of Britain ace Wg Cdr Joe Kayll, described;

'I was to lead the Escort Wing but at the last moment Gp Capt Broadhurst (Station Commander RAF Hornchurch) said that he would like to lead so I decided to go as his No 2. The raid was carried out successfully and the Wing headed for home, but Gp Capt Broadhurst decided to fly back over France. He detached the leading flight of four aircraft and headed west, climbing to gain height. While still climbing steeply, we were attacked by Me 109s from out of the sun – Nos 3 and 4 were shot down and did not survive. Gp Capt Broadhurst managed to get back to the UK but I was hit in the engine and lost all power. I was not able to jump as any attempt to slow down was an invitation for further attacks, so I landed wheels up in a pea field between two canals and was captured hiding in a cornfield after about 30 minutes. We were an easy target and I was lucky to survive.'

In the same action Flt Lt Roy Mottram of No 54 Sqn shot down a Bf 109, and was thus elevated to ace status, whilst Wg Cdr Douglas Bader, leading the Tangmere Wing, also got a Bf 109 near Boulogne and shared a second with future ace Sgt Jeff West of No 616 Sqn. No 92 Sqn's Plt Off Neville Duke was also in action, and in his diary he vividly described the first of his 28 victories;

'Allan and self dived down on two '109s over St Omer – couldn't catch them – going at a phenomenal airspeed. '109s pulled up vertically. I blacked out and broke away, just avoiding stalling. Saw Allan [Battle of Britain ace Flg Off Allan Wright] and '109 diving, with glycol pouring from '109.

'I was attacked by two '109s from astern but saw them just in time and did a terrific turn, seeing tracer whistle past behind. Came out over Dunkirk and passed two '109s on way. Turned and saw dogfight going on near Dunkirk, so went back and joined in. Sat on the tail of a '109 which was shooting at another Spit. Fired several bursts of cannon and machine gun into him from about 50 yards' range. Glycol streamed out and he started going down. Got just above him and looked down into his cockpit. Pilot was crouched over stick and did not look up. Think perhaps I hit him. The '109 went down and crashed a few miles inland. Sped home at sea level at terrific bat. Engine stopped just as I touched down on 'drome for lack of petrol!'

The next day (26 June) Sgt 'Bill' Johnson of No 145 Sqn also began his path to acedom, noting in his log book, 'Medium cover Dunkirk-St Omer. Me 109F destroyed. Sgt [A] Macbeth missing (PoW)'. The following day No 266 Sqn flew its first 'Circus', during which Sgt Lewis destroyed a Bf 109 but Plt Offs S Cook and W H Holland were lost. In that same action No 19 Sqn's Battle of Britain ace Flt Lt Walter Lawson had made a quarter attack on a Bf 109E at the rear of a formation of enemy fighters engaged about ten miles east of St Omer. The Messerschmitt pulled up and stalled as glycol vapour poured from under the wings, the fighter then falling away in a spiral dive before flames enveloped the fuselage – it was Lawson's final victory, and shortly thereafter he assumed command of No 19 Sqn.

Also successful was Sgt David Cox (flying P8460/QV-L), who, many years later, described his fourth victory to the author;

'I managed to get behind four '109s at something over 20,000 ft and went for the rear one. I must have fired at least a couple of bursts as I closed in, and these resulted in some flames coming out from it. It went over and down vertically, wrapped up in flames. I looked for the rest of the squadron and was about to join what I thought was a formation of Spits when I saw streams of tracer coming past me on the left and hitting my wing. They must have hit the glycol tank, as having managed to evade this unwelcome intruder my engine failed and I just managed to glide back to crash land on the Kent coast. By such small margins!'

In early June No 266 Sqn's CO 'Jamie' Jameson had become the Wittering Wing Leader, with command of the unit having then passed to Sqn Ldr Tristram 'Tommy' Beresford, an experienced pre-war regular who had received a DFC for his actions over Waziristan in 1938.

THE ACES FALL

The heavy fighting also saw No 74 Sqn suffer a severe blow on 27 June when its CO, 23-year-old Sqn Ldr John Mungo-Park (flying X4668/ZP-E), was shot down and killed. His unit had engaged two formations of Bf 109s led by *experten* Hauptmann Wilhelm Balthazar, *Geschwaderkommodore* of JG 2, and Hauptmann Rolf Pingel, *Gruppenkommandeur* of I./JG 26. Covering the formation as 'tail end Charlie' was Sgt Clive Hilken, who described the fight in which his CO was killed;

'At 2500 ft over France our squadron became separated on a weaving turn from the other squadrons of the Wing. Our CO applied full throttle in an attempt to regain his place in the formation but in the process the rest of us found ourselves spread over the sky up to two miles behind the main formation. Now, to weave and watch your tail meant losing the formation. The only way to catch up was to do what our CO had done – full bore.

'I was attacked and hit by cannon shells from below and on the starboard side. I pulled round to port and yelled into the radio but it was dead, and I could see that my Spitfire was spewing out a white trail and couldn't see the attackers. I can only presume that they came out of the sun and attacked from below to take out Plt Off [W J] Sandman and Sqn Ldr Mungo-Park.'

No 74 Sqn suffered a severe blow on 27 June 1941 when its CO, 23-year-old Sqn Ldr John Mungo-Park (flying X4668/ZP-E), was shot down and killed. His unit had engaged two formations of Bf 109s led by *experten* Hauptmann Wilhelm Balthazar, *Geschwaderkommodore* of JG 2, and Hauptmann Rolf Pingel, *Gruppenkommandeur* of I./JG 26. The shattered remains of X4668 are seen here being picked over by the Wehrmacht where it fell near Adinkerke, in western Belgium (*via Chris Goss*)

The momentous month ended when, during an evening sweep over northern France, Malan's Wing was in action, with its dynamic leader claiming his 29th success with the demise of a Bf 109 west of Lille. No 609 Sqn's pilots claimed three more, including one to Belgian Plt Off 'Vicky' Ortmans who thus became an ace. Further west, No 66 Sqn's Flt Lt 'Dizzy' Allen claimed his final victories when, over the Channel south of Bolt Head, he shared a Bf 109 and soon after got another off Plymouth, taking his total to eight.

The hectic pace of operations continued into July, and it was to be maintained throughout the summer. This in turn meant that Fighter Command suffered a continual drain on experienced pilots, many of them aces. During a 'Circus' to Lille on 2 July Flt Sgt Don Kingaby executed a remarkable double victory;

'I had one of the luckiest shots at a Hun I can ever remember. We were just crossing the French coast on the way home when I decided to take a chance this time and take a quick squirt at the first one I saw. I broke away and climbed immediately to throw the '109's pals off the scent. No 2 called up on the R/T to say that I had got two of them. Apparently I hit the first one and the second collided with him. I looked down and there were two parachutes and then two great splashes as the remains of their machines hit the drink.'

Also claiming a pair of Bf 109s that same day was future ace Sgt Larry Robillard of No 145 Sqn, who saw a parachute descending that he believed (in error) was that of his CO, and fellow Canadian, Sqn Ldr Stan Turner. When covering the descent, he was attacked by nine Bf 109s, two of which he managed to shoot down before he was himself shot down in P8536/SO-B. Evading capture, Robillard escaped via Spain to Gibraltar – he later received a DFM for his actions on this day. However, his ace flight commander, Flt Lt Mike Newling, was not so fortunate four days later when, over Lille, he was shot down and killed in Spitfire VA W3366.

The beginning of July was also significant for No 266 Sqn as on the afternoon of the 3rd it flew its first operation as a 'Rhodesian' unit, during which Tommy Beresford shot down a Bf 109 – the first of his eventual five victories;

'I suddenly saw 18 Me 109s flying across my bows at 45 degrees. The Squadron immediately attacked and after breaking them up we were in turn attacked by another 12 Me 109s also flying in the same direction as the previous lot. The dogfight resolved itself into a confused affair, with aircraft fighting in pairs and pilots breaking off the fight as the odds became too heavy, returning to base in ones and twos. Of the 12 Me 109s sighted slightly to port, I singled out the righthand one which was lagging and got onto his tail. I gave him a five-second burst from 200 yards, closing to 100 yards, and saw him dive vertically down smoking. Sgt Devenish saw this aircraft hit the ground.'

A day of heavy fighting saw the death of Hauptmann Wilhelm Balthazar, *Geschwaderkommodore* of JG 2, when the wing of his Bf 109F detached as he performed a spiral dive, possibly as a result of damage inflicted by No 609 Sqn's CO, Sqn Ldr Michael Lister-Robinson. On 4 July the Hornchurch Station Commander, Gp Capt Harry Broadhurst, was wounded during a 'Circus', whilst Canadian Flt Lt Keith Ogilvie of

No 609 Sqn, who had become an ace just two weeks earlier, was shot down by JG 26 and bailed out wounded to become a PoW. However, No 611 Sqn's Sgt 'Mac' Gilmour – known as 'that elongated Scot' – shot down a Bf 109 at 10,000 ft over St Omer;

'I closed to 250-300 yards, using both cannon and machine guns. There was a great flash from his tail unit and bits of aircraft fell around. I had started my attack at 10,000 ft and finally broke away at about 6000 ft. The Me 109 was then going vertically downward, and it went into cloud (3000 ft) in this attitude.'

Gilmour's fourth victory was witnessed by Flt Lt Eric Lock. However, No 603 Sqn's promising Flg Off Harry Prowse, who had three victories, was hit by flak that same day when strafing St Omer airfield and became a PoW.

'Circus 33' on 5 July, targeting the steel works at Lille, was significant as it was the first daylight mission involving the RAF's new four-engined Short Stirling heavy bombers. Although three Spitfires were lost defending the aircraft, Flt Lt 'Hawkeye' Wells of No 485 Sqn (in Spitfire II P8022) shot down two Bf 109s in a little over five minutes to become the first pilot to be elevated to ace whilst serving with the New Zealand-manned unit. Lille was again the target for Stirlings on 6 July, as No 611 Sqn's diarist noted. 'Even Göring would have been amazed by the number of medals worn by the pilots of "Charlie" Section! This comprised Flt Lt Lock DSO DFC, Flg Off Dexter DFC, Plt Off Duncan-Smith DFC and Sgt Gilmour DFM'. Lock claimed one destroyed while Gilmour, who was attacked by four Messerschmitts, claimed another to become an ace. Finally, Gp Capt Harry Broadhurst, who was flying with No 611 Sqn, also claimed two Bf 109s during the course of this action.

Sqn Ldr Ken Holden, CO of No 610 Sqn, 'made ace' during 'Circus 33' when he shot down a Bf 109E. Minutes later he shared in the destruction of another one with Australian Plt Off Tony Gaze, this being the future ace's second victory. However, on the debit side, the following day another ace

One of the leading pilots of the Battle of Britain, Flt Lt Eric Lock joined No 611 Sqn after spending eight months recovering from wounds to his right arm and both legs inflicted by a Bf 109E from JG 54 that jumped him shortly after he had claimed his 23rd victory on 17 November 1940. Lock joined his new unit as a flight commander, flying suitably marked Spitfire VB W3257/FY-E (*A P Fergusson*)

fell when No 74 Sqn's Plt Off Bill Skinner was shot down whilst escorting a Stirling raid and he became a PoW. Having suffered heavy losses in recent weeks, No 74 Sqn was replaced at Gravesend on 6 July by No 72 Sqn, which was under the command of Battle of Britain ace Sqn Ldr Des Sheen.

That same day (6 July), during a sweep near Dunkirk, Flg Off Peter Dexter of No 611 Sqn, who was originally a Lysander army cooperation pilot, shot down a Bf 109 to become an ace. His victim may have been Unteroffizier Albrecht Held of 1./JG 26, who was killed in Bf 109F Wk-Nr 9157.

Action for the Spitfire units came not only over France, however, as on 7/8 July No 118 Sqn mounted a number of 'Fighter Night' patrols. During the early hours of the 8th unit CO Sqn Ldr Frank Howell spotted a He 111 over Southampton. His second attack resulted in what he described as 'a mother and father of an explosion on the Heinkel'. With the He 111's port engine ablaze, the bomber fell rapidly away streaming smoke until it eventually ditched south of Worthing, with its crew becoming PoWs. Frank Howell's eighth victory was also No 118 Sqn's first. That same night Sqn Ldr Adrian Boyd claimed No 501 Sqn's first Spitfire victory when, near Portsmouth, he found a Ju 88 and shot it down for his 16th success.

A few hours later, during an early morning 'Circus' west of Lens, Sgt David Hughes-Rees (in W3239/PR-N) shot down a Bf 109 to become an ace. He was awarded a DFM the next month and later moved to the Middle East where, sadly, he succumbed to polio. No 611 Sqn was active again that same day when, flying W3242/FY-N *Crispin of Leicester*, which also carried his personal name *Atchashikar* (Hindi for 'Good Hunting'), Plt Off Duncan-Smith achieved acedom, as he described in his autobiography;

'I got behind the last one and opened fire. The muffled boom-boom from the cannons was a welcome new sound, but the orange flash from one of my cannon shells, quite vivid as it exploded against the enemy's cockpit cover, was even more startling. Closing, I fired a second burst, but my Spitfire pitched and yawed away from my line of sight. In a split second the '109 rolled onto its back, diving steeply with smoke pouring from a hit in the cooling system.'

Then at lunchtime on 9 July, when No 54 Sqn was in combat in the St Omer area, Flg Off 'Jack' Charles achieved acedom when he shot down a Bf 109F. More established pilots also hit their stride at this time, with No 501 Sqn's Flt Lt 'Ginger' Lacey claiming his first Spitfire victory on the 10th whilst escorting Blenheims attacking Cherbourg. Having spotted two Bf 109s diving down as they approached the coast, the high-scoring Battle of Britain ace quickly shot one of them down for his 24th victory – Lacey's last success had come on 30 October 1940. A week later, when to the south of Portland, he shot down a Heinkel He 59 floatplane.

New units continued to become operational with the Spitfire during the summer of 1941, among them No 452 Sqn – the first Spitfire unit of the Royal Australian Air Force (RAAF). The squadron flew its first sweep on 11 July, during which Flt Lt 'Paddy' Finucane shot down a Bf 109;

'I cut on the inside of his turn and followed him down. When about 150 yards behind I gave him a short burst of three seconds. The enemy pilot bailed out.'

The Irishman had used just 90 rounds to claim the squadron's first victory. However, aces continued to fall, with No 54 Sqn's Flt Lt Peter

Kiwi Sqn Ldr Vaughan Minden Blake had flown throughout the Battle of Britain (with No 238 Sqn) and continued to make claims in 1941 as CO of No 234 Sqn. On 10 July 1941, having downed two Bf 109s, he was then forced to ditch close to the French coast. Unperturbed, Minden Blake paddled for 12 hours to reach safety (*via N L R Franks*)

The blazing wreckage of this No 611 Sqn Spitfire VB is believed to be Flt Lt Eric Lock's W3257, in which he was shot down during a strafing attack on German troops near Calais on 3 August 1941 (*A P Fergusson*)

Gardner being shot down and wounded to become a PoW that same day. Then, during a 'Circus' on the morning of 14 July over Boulogne, South African ace Flt Lt Peter Dexter of No 611 Sqn collided with another Spitfire from No 54 Sqn. Although both pilots bailed out, Dexter was killed, possibly by having struck his aircraft as he exited the cockpit. Ten days later 20-year-old Flt Lt 'Boy' Marrs of No 152 Sqn, who had claimed his 13th victory on 18 July, was shot down by flak and killed while escorting Hampden bombers targeting German battleships in Brest harbour.

Despite the high attrition rate pilots continued to reach acedom, with No 616 Sqn's Flg Off 'Cocky' Dundas claiming his all important fifth success on 19 July when, in a day of heavy fighting, he shared a Bf 109 with Douglas Bader. Two days later Wg Cdr 'Eric' Stapleton shot down a pair of Bf 109s over Lille, taking the veteran 29-year-old Hornchurch Wing Leader to acedom. Then, during an evening sweep on the 23rd by No 616 Sqn, the Bf 109 that fell to the guns of Flt Lt 'Buck' Casson also made him an ace. The Australians in No 452 Sqn saw more action the following day when Flg Off Andrew Humphrey shot down a Bf 109 north of Cherbourg whilst returning from an operation, so taking him to acedom – the first pilot from the unit to do so. Humphrey later rose to become Chief of the Air Staff of the RAF in 1974. He was the last Spitfire ace to hold that position.

August opened with the loss of a further leading pilot when, during a 'Rhubarb' on the 3rd, Flt Lt Eric Lock, who had 26 victories to his name, was killed when strafing troops near Calais in W3257/FY-E. Flt Lt Wilf Duncan-Smith said of his friend, 'He was quite a chum and a remarkable bloke altogether. He was an excellent shot with an aerial gun'. Another of his contemporaries recalled that 'he had courage – a pint-sized pilot with gallons of courage, and a great pilot'. Worse followed six days later when ten Spitfires were lost, among them the aircraft flown by the Tangmere Wing Leader, Wg Cdr Douglas Bader. He collided with a Bf 109 and had to bail out of W3185/DB. Fellow ace Flt Lt 'Buck' Casson of No 616 Sqn also bailed out, having possibly fallen victim to *experte* Hauptmann Gerhard Schöpfel, *Gruppenkommandeur* of III./JG 26, who claimed two kills to take his tally to 32. On a more positive note, Plt Off 'Johnnie' Johnson (in W3334) shot down a Bf 109 and soon after shared in the destruction of a second, taking him to acedom.

In a torrid day for Fighter Command, No 92 Sqn's Plt Off Neville Duke claimed his second victory, although he noted, 'Chased to within 2-3 miles of Dover by two '109s. Damned lucky to be alive. God, what a life!' Nevertheless, this and other successes during the summer of 1941 cemented No 92 Sqn's position as Fighter Command's leading unit in terms of aerial victories.

During the night Blitz 'Fighter Night' patrols by Spitfires met with occasional success, with Wittering-based No 266 Sqn achieving a number of victories. During May 1941 Plt Off Andrew Humphrey shot down three He 111s at night – a remarkable feat. He later rose through the ranks to become the Chief of the Air Staff (*MoD*)

Despite considerable losses, the RAF fighters were meeting the Luftwaffe on equal terms, although this situation was soon to change dramatically. Operations continued through August, again with steady losses but also with a number of pilots adding to their scores as they neared acedom. Among them were South African Flg Off 'Chris' Le Roux of No 91 Sqn, Flt Lt David Scott-Malden of No 603 Sqn and No 609 Sqn's Plt Off Yvan du Monceau de Bergendael from Belgium, who wrote in his log book;

'Me 109Es weaving behind, left French coast north of Boulogne and passed 1000 ft above me. Me 109Es had yellow noses. Climbed into sun. Attacked No 1 aircraft after scaring Nos 3 and 4 off. One Me 109E destroyed, down off Calais.'

However, on the debit side, among those lost was No 610 Sqn's Flt Lt Denis Crowley-Milling on 20 August, although he evaded capture and eventually returned in 1942. His was one of 17 Spitfires downed that day, following on from 12 lost 24 hours earlier. On the 28th more aces fell when No 19 Sqn's 28-year-old CO Sqn Ldr Walter Lawson was lost off Rotterdam, whilst squadronmate Flt Lt 'Jock' Cunningham became a PoW. Worse was to follow during a search for the CO the next morning, when No 19 Sqn was hit by ten Bf 110s of 6./ZG 76 and four pilots were lost. A bad month ended with the loss of the North Weald Wing Leader, Wg Cdr John Gillan, also on the 29th, and No 54 Sqn ace Flt Lt Roy Mottram on the 31st.

However, RAF pilots continued hitting the enemy too, including future ace Flg Off Peter Howard-Williams of No 118 Sqn, who, on 3 September attacked an E-boat off Cherbourg;

'I led the attack on the E-boat, and it was soon stopped in the water. We all made two attacks and it was soon a right mess, with smoke pouring from it when we set course for home. Later, the Germans announced that the Commander-in-Chief of all the western defences had been killed at sea. We put in a claim for one Field Marshal destroyed!'

The following day future ace Sgt Deryck Lamb of No 603 Sqn fielded a more conventional claim when, off Dunkirk, in combat with Bf 109s of JG 26 he shot one down for his first victory;

'The '109 apparently did not see me as I turned left and got right onto his tail, catching him up very easily. I opened fire and closed to 50 yards, giving him a five-second burst of cannon and machine gun fire. He did not pull out but went straight into a field about five miles south-southeast of Dunkerque. There was a flash and a cloud of black smoke and he just "splattered" over the field.' *(Text continues on page 45.)*

Flg Off 'Buck' Casson (centre) poses for a photograph with his groundcrew at Tangmere. He was shot down and became a PoW on 9 August 1941 in the same combat as his Wing Leader, Wg Cdr Douglas Bader (*L H Casson via G R Pitchfork*)

COLOUR PLATES

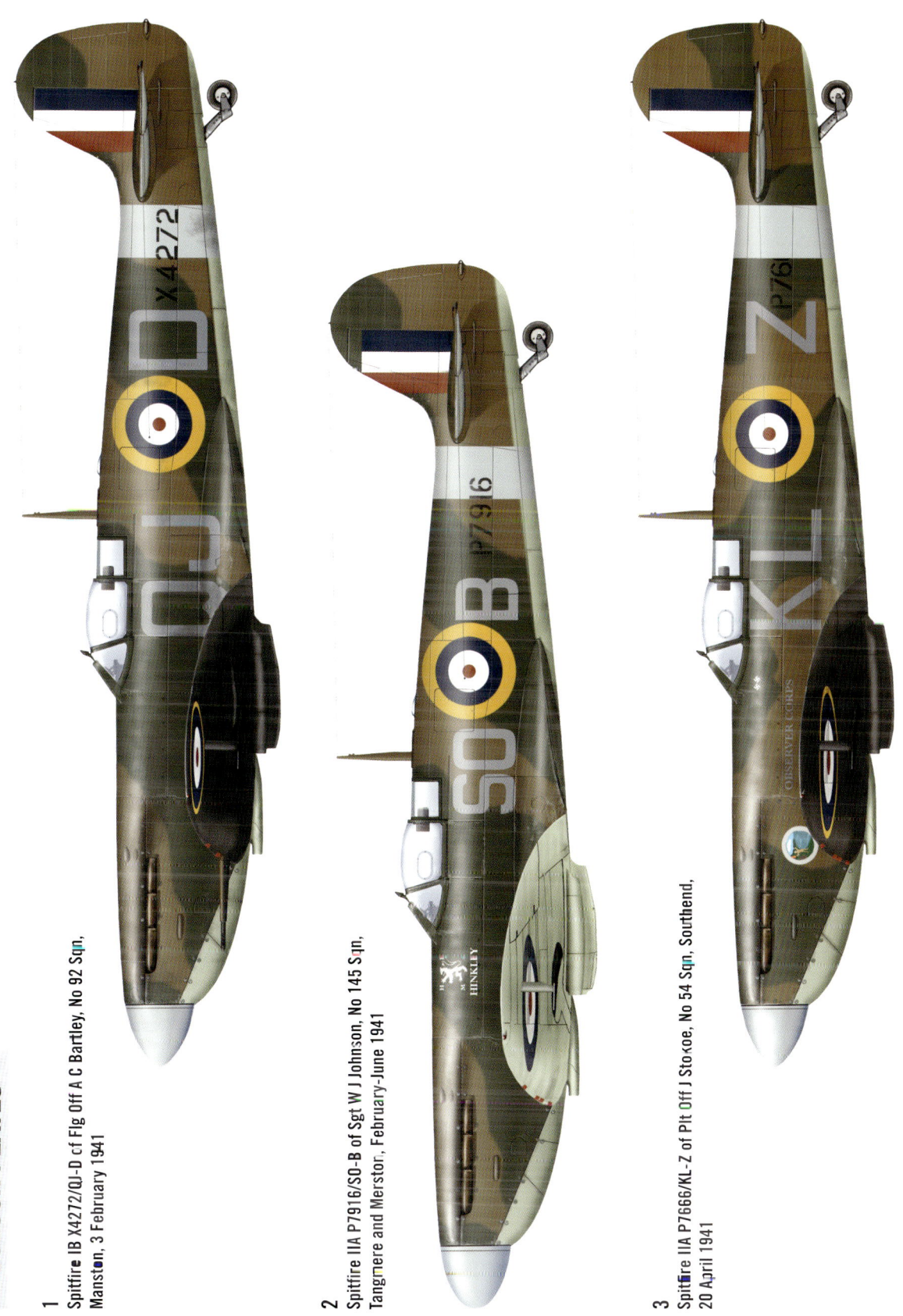

1
Spitfire IB X4272/QJ-D of Flg Off A C Bartley, No 92 Sqn, Manston, 3 February 1941

2
Spitfire IIA P7916/SO-B of Sgt W J Johnson, No 145 Sqn, Tangmere and Merston, February-June 1941

3
Spitfire IIA P7666/KL-Z of Plt Off J Stokoe, No 54 Sqn, Southend, 20 April 1941

4
Spitfire IIA P7753/QJ-X of Flg Off L H Casson, No 616 'South Yorkshire' Sqn, Tangmere, 5 May 1941

5
Spitfire IIA P8376/NK-Z of Flg Off P I Howard-Williams, No 118 Sqn, Ibsley, May-June 1941

6
Spitfire VB P8749/DW-G of Flg Off F A O Gaze, No 610 'County of Chester' Sqn, Westhampnet, 10 July 1941

7
Spitfire VB W3380/RN-J of Sqn Ldr D F B Sheen, No 72 Sqn, Gravesend and Biggin Hill, July-October 1941

8
Spitfire VB W3628/XT-P of Sgt D P Lamb, No 603 'City of Edinburgh' Sqn, Hornchurch, August-September 1941

9
Spitfire VB W3579/OU-Q of Flt Lt S C Norris, No 485 Sqn RNZAF, Redhill and Kenley, August-October 1941

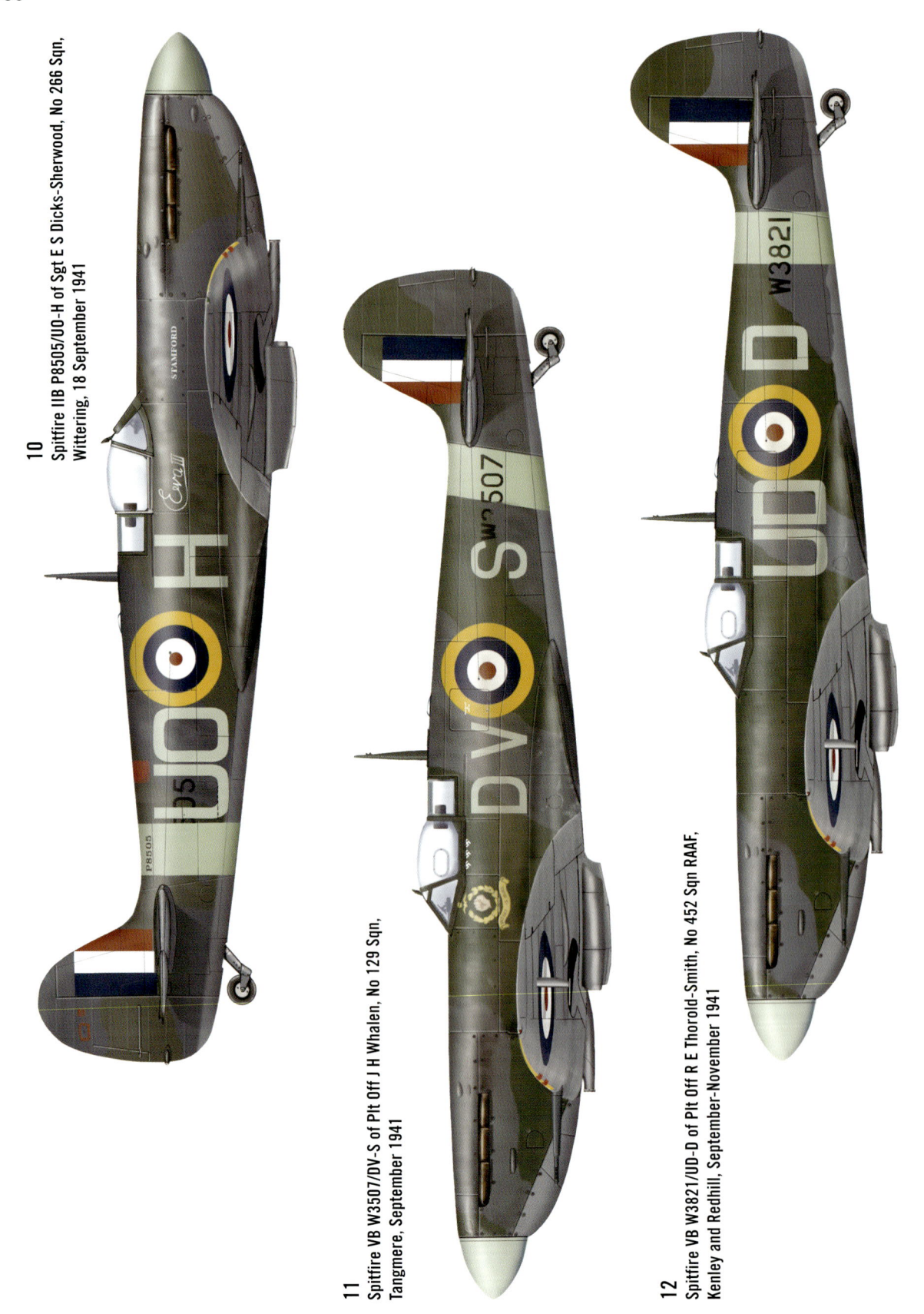

10
Spitfire IIB P8505/UO-H of Sgt E S Dicks-Sherwood, No 266 Sqn, Wittering, 18 September 1941

11
Spitfire VB W3507/DV-S of Plt Off J H Whalen, No 129 Sqn, Tangmere, September 1941

12
Spitfire VB W3821/UO-D of Plt Off R E Thorold-Smith, No 452 Sqn RAAF, Kenley and Redhill, September-November 1941

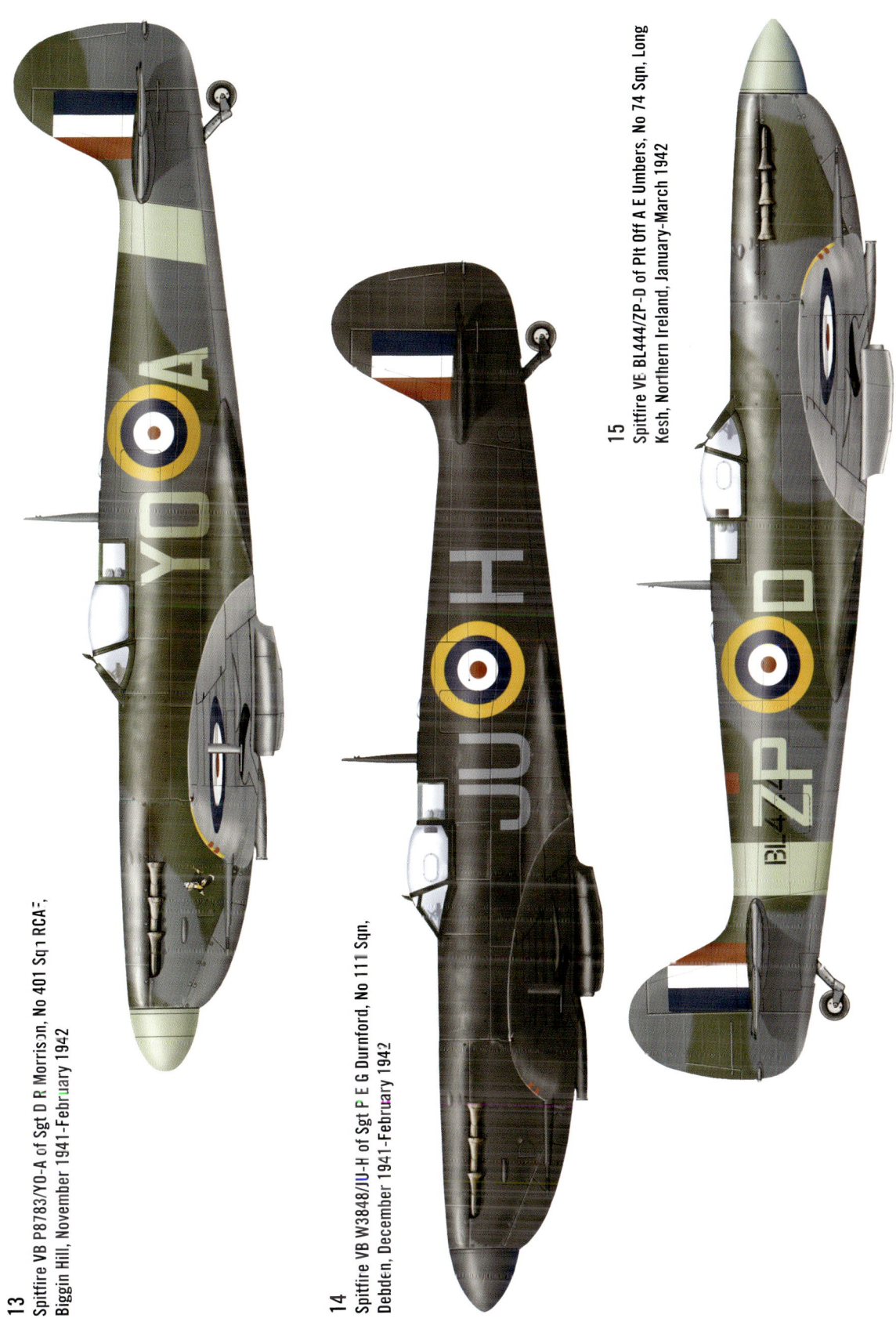

13
Spitfire VB P8783/YO-A of Sgt D R Morrison, No 401 Sqn RCAF, Biggin Hill, November 1941-February 1942

14
Spitfire VB W3848/JU-H of Sgt P E G Durnford, No 111 Sqn, Debden, December 1941-February 1942

15
Spitfire VE BL444/ZP-D of Plt Off A E Umbers, No 74 Sqn, Long Kesh, Northern Ireland, January-March 1942

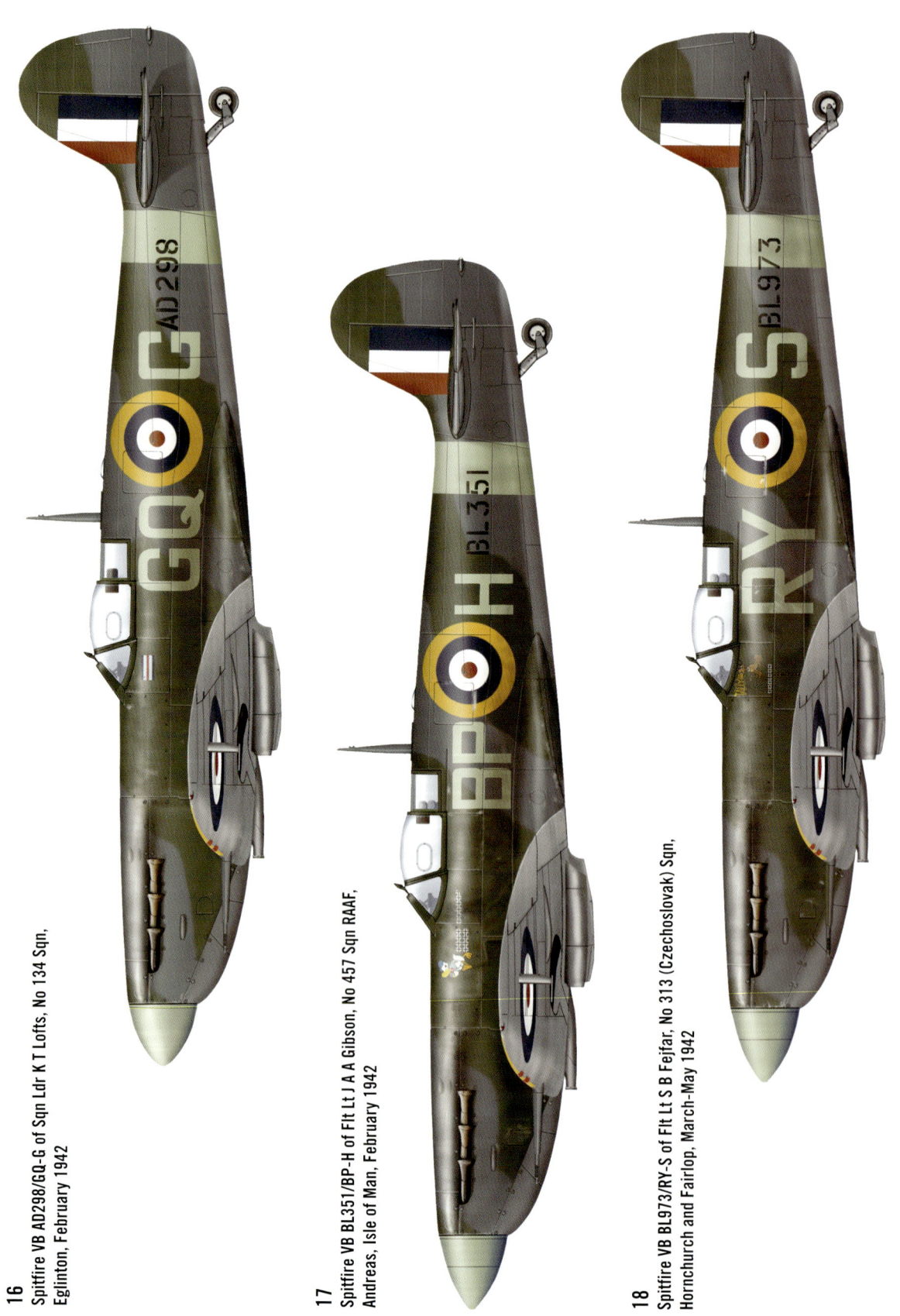

16
Spitfire VB AD298/GQ-G of Sqn Ldr K T Lofts, No 134 Sqn,
Eglinton, February 1942

17
Spitfire VB BL351/BP-H of Flt Lt J A A Gibson, No 457 Sqn RAAF,
Andreas, Isle of Man, February 1942

18
Spitfire VB BL973/RY-S of Flt Lt S B Fejfar, No 313 (Czechoslovak) Sqn,
Hornchurch and Fairlop, March-May 1942

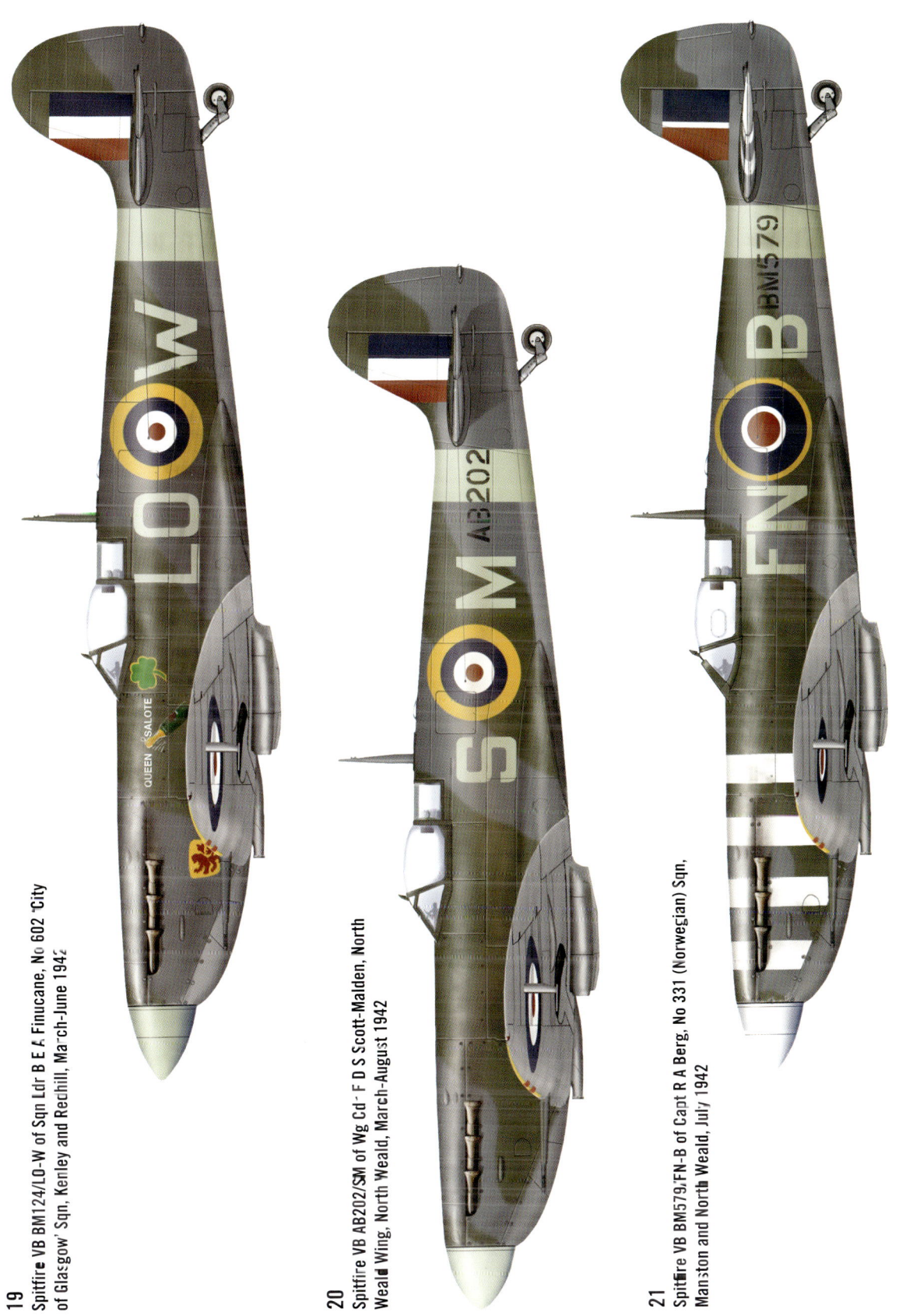

19
Spitfire VB BM124/LO-W of Sqn Ldr B E A Finucane, No 602 'City of Glasgow' Sqn, Kenley and Redhill, March-June 1942

20
Spitfire VB AB202/SM of Wg Cdr F D S Scott-Malden, North Weald Wing, North Weald, March-August 1942

21
Spitfire VB BM579/FN-B of Capt R A Berg, No 331 (Norwegian) Sqn, Manston and North Weald, July 1942

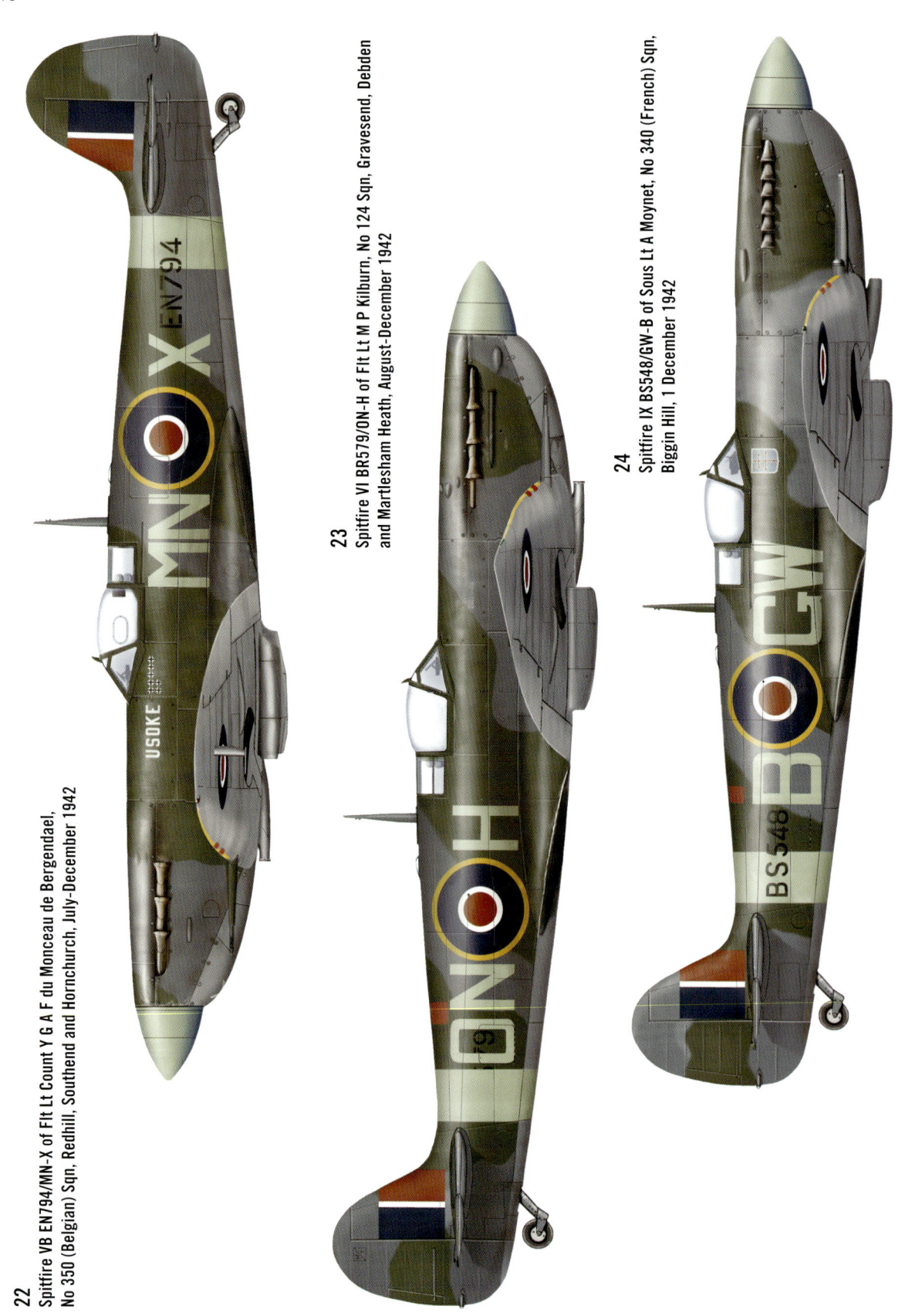

22
Spitfire VB EN794/MN-X of Flt Lt Count Y G A F du Monceau de Bergendael,
No 350 (Belgian) Sqn, Redhill, Southend and Hornchurch, July–December 1942

23
Spitfire VI BR579/ON-H of Flt Lt M P Kilburn, No 124 Sqn, Gravesend, Debden
and Martlesham Heath, August–December 1942

24
Spitfire IX BS548/GW-B of Sous Lt A Moynet, No 340 (French) Sqn,
Biggin Hill, 1 December 1942

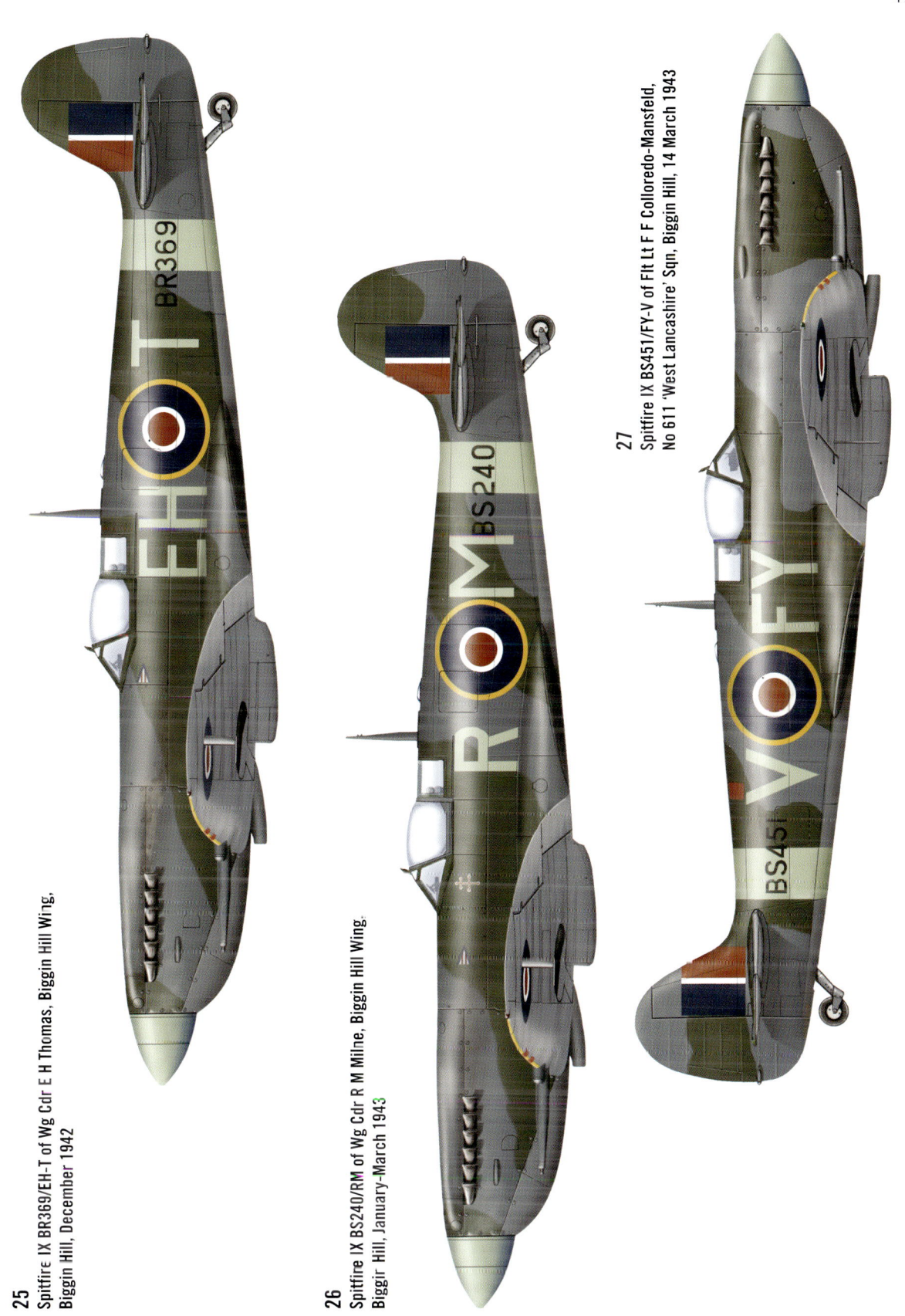

25
Spitfire IX BR369/EH-T of Wg Cdr E H Thomas, Biggin Hill Wing, Biggin Hill, December 1942

26
Spitfire IX BS240/RM of Wg Cdr R M Milne, Biggin Hill Wing, Biggin Hill, January–March 1943

27
Spitfire IX BS451/FY-V of Flt Lt F F Colloredo-Mansfeld, No 611 'West Lancashire' Sqn, Biggin Hill, 14 March 1943

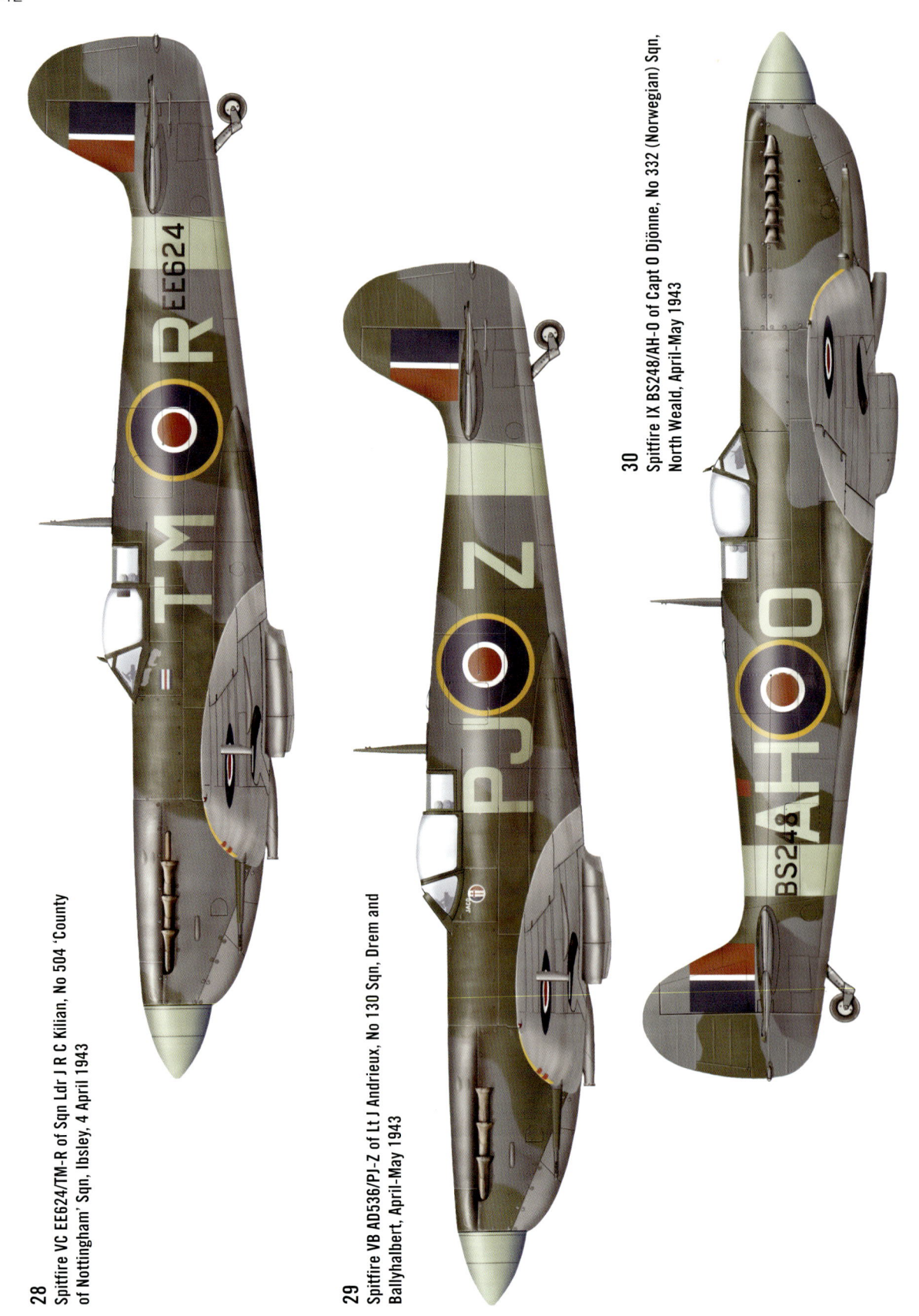

28
Spitfire VC EE624/TM-R of Sqn Ldr J R C Kilian, No 504 'County of Nottingham' Sqn, Ibsley, 4 April 1943

29
Spitfire VB AD536/PJ-Z of Lt J Andrieux, No 130 Sqn, Drem and Ballyhalbert, April-May 1943

30
Spitfire IX BS248/AH-O of Capt O Djönne, No 332 (Norwegian) Sqn, North Weald, April-May 1943

43

31
Spitfire IX LZ997/KH-A of Flt Lt W A Conrad, No 403 Sqn RCAF, Lashenden and Headcorn, June-August 1943.

32
Spitfire IX MH434/ZD-B of Flt Lt H P Lardner-Burke, No 222 Sqn, Hornchurch August-September 1943

33
Spitfire VB BM515/VL-P of Flg Off J L Plesman, No 322 (Dutch) Sqn, Llanbedr and Woodvale, August-December 1943

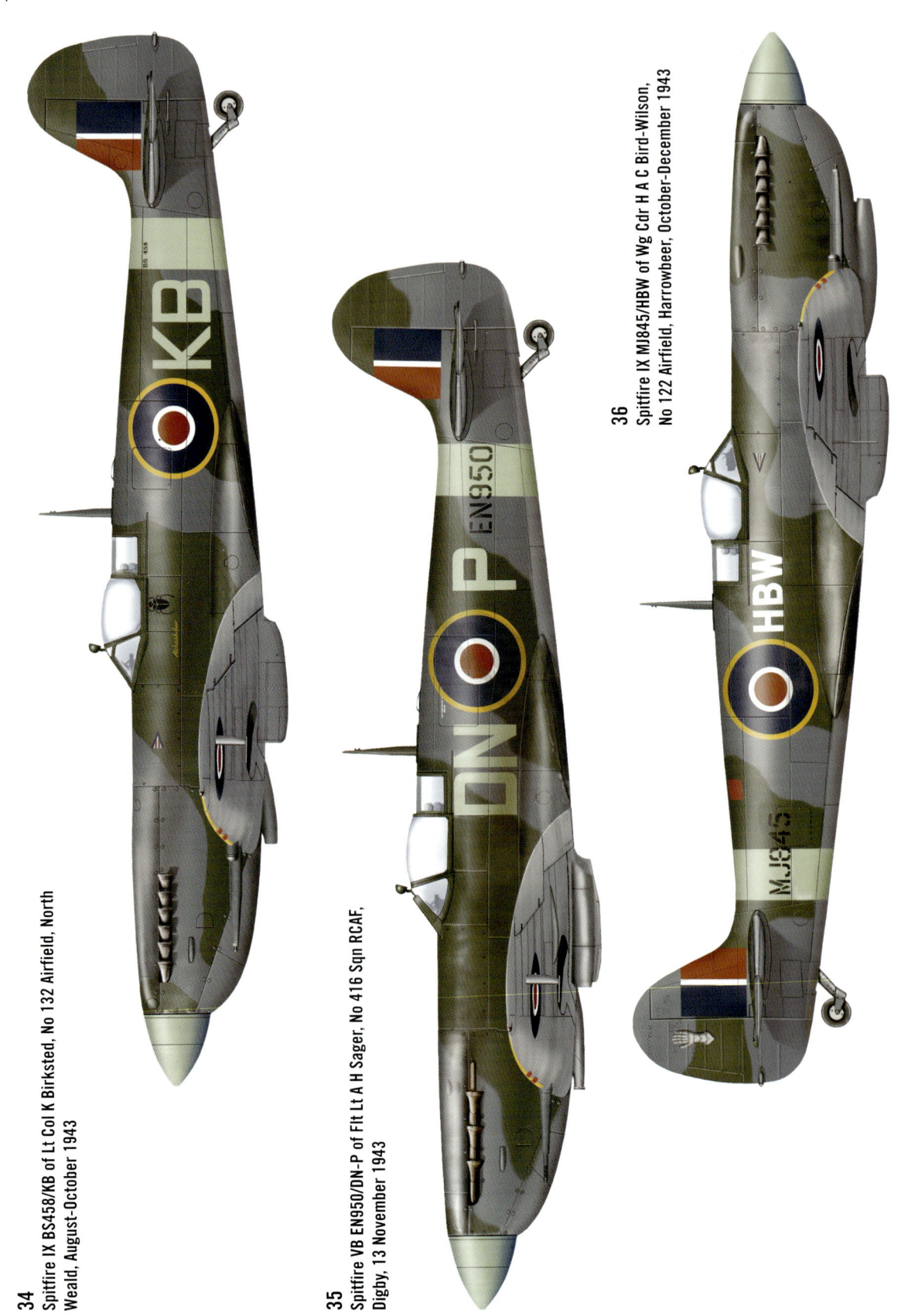

34
Spitfire IX BS458/KB of Lt Col K Birksted, No 132 Airfield, North Weald, August–October 1943

35
Spitfire VB EN950/DN-P of Flt Lt A H Sager, No 416 Sqn RCAF, Digby, 13 November 1943

36
Spitfire IX MJ845/HBW of Wg Cdr H A C Bird-Wilson, No 122 Airfield, Harrowbeer, October–December 1943

ENTER THE 'BUTCHER BIRD'

An encounter on 18 September during a sweep by 12 Spitfires of No 41 Sqn resulted in some unusual claims, one of which was to prove ominously significant. At 1030 hrs over Ostend, New Zealander Flt Lt Roy Bush and Rhodesian Plt Off 'Buck' Buchanan shot down an Hs 123 biplane to give the latter his first success, whilst Flt Lt Roy Marples and Plt Off Geoff Ranger destroyed a hapless Junkers W 34 over the Belgian town. This was Ranger's second victory, but the share gave Marples ace status. Battle of Britain ace Plt Off Cyril Babbage also claimed an unusual type off Ostend;

'This enemy aircraft appeared to be similar to a Curtiss 75A but with a slimmer fuselage. Enemy aircraft passed beneath me and I saw crosses on the fuselage. It then turned south at high speed and I followed it at 12½ lbs boost and 2800 revs, with the result that I was overhauling slowly indicated airspeed 350 mph at sea level. I got within range just off Ostend and fired a five-second burst from dead astern. Enemy aircraft broke up and crashed into sea.'

Babbage's victim was in fact one of the first pre-production Focke-Wulf Fw 190s to reach the frontline, the fighter being flown by 25-victory *experte* Hauptmann Walter Adolph, *Gruppenkommodore* II./JG 26 and holder of the Knight's Cross, who was killed. Babbage's significant, if at the time unrecognised, final victory was the first Fw 190 confirmed destroyed. Ominously for Fighter Command the 'Butcher Bird' had arrived, which at a stroke outclassed the RAF's fighter mainstay the Spitfire V.

The Fw 190 was then encountered occasionally, the fighter continuing to cause confusion as to its identity. For example, when No 603 Sqn engaged the aeroplane near St Omer on 27 September, the radial-engined fighter was variously reported as a captured French Curtiss Hawk or Bloch MB 152. One was claimed shot down by Sgt Dalton Prytherch for his second victory. Flt Lt Wilf Duncan-Smith recalled, 'I suddenly noticed a radial-engined aircraft diving through the formation. I thought I was seeing things'. Later, he wrote in his log book in red ink, 'First contact with FW 190'. A Polish pilot claimed another later that same day (27th), although he identified it as a 'Macchi 200'!

Returning to 18 September, another significant event occurred on this date when, during a 'Circus' to Rouen, Sgt Keith Chisholm of No 452 Sqn become the first Australian in an RAAF Spitfire squadron to become an ace. Two days later, 25 year-old Victorian Plt Off 'Bluey' Truscott shot down two Bf 109s to become the latest RAAF ace. Both he and Chisholm were decorated (the latter receiving

On 18 September 1941 Plt Off Cyril Babbage of No 41 Sqn shot down a radial-engined fighter to claim his eighth, and most significant, victory. The aeroplane was flown by the *experte* Hauptmann Walter Adolf, the *Gruppenkommandeur* of II./JG 26, who was at the controls of the first Focke-Wulf Fw 190 to be downed (*via Robert Forsyth*)

Coming over the hedge at Kenley in the summer of 1941 is Spitfire IIA P7786/UD-C of No 452 Sqn. On 9 August it was flown by Sgt Keith Chisholm when he shared in the destruction of two Bf 109s. Chisholm would subsequently become the first RAAF ace over the Channel Front (*J D R Rawlings*)

a DFM), as was 'Paddy' Finucane, who received the DSO. However, Chisholm was shot down over the Channel and captured soon afterwards.

As autumn approached at Ibsley, both Nos 118 and 501 Sqns were used in the making of the film *First of the Few*, during which, on 9 October, the latter unit was scrambled to intercept an unfortunate Ju 88 south of Portland Bill. All the pilots involved fired at it before the bomber went down, the CO, Sqn Ldr 'Bunny' Currant, remarking, 'the weight of lead from 12 Spitfires being too much to carry!'

Offensive operations continued, and during a sweep over the Pas de Calais area four days later the recently formed Canadian No 411 Sqn became engaged with Bf 109s. Plt Off 'Buck' McNair achieved the first of his 16 victories when he shot one down off Boulogne, although his fighter was also hit. Forced to bail out, the future ace was rescued by the Royal Navy. No 452 Sqn was also in action that day (13 October), claiming six destroyed. Amongst the successful pilots was Flg Off 'Throttle' Thorold-Smith, who became an ace, whilst 'Bluey' Truscott also increased his score.

Others continued to claim victories throughout the month, although at an increasing cost. For example, on the 27th, No 401 Sqn suffered heavily at the hands of I. and III./JG 26 over Gravelines, losing four pilots – Oberstleutnant Adolf Galland claimed his 93rd victory and Hauptmann 'Pips' Priller his 56th during this action. A 'Circus' on the 31st saw the demise of yet another Wing Leader when Wg Cdr Norman Ryder of the Kenley Wing, flying with No 485 Sqn, was shot down by flak and became a PoW. In early November, Flt Lt Finucane of No 452 Sqn, having shot down a brace of Fw 190s, was forced to bail out, although he was rescued. However, losses continued to increase, and the destruction of 17 Spitfires during a 'Circus' against Lille on 8 November, combined with the perceived threat of the Fw 190, resulted in the suspension of the 1941 'non-stop' offensive on the 13th. Some smaller-scale sweeps continued through the deteriorating winter weather, although at a much lower rate.

Home defence against enemy intruders remained undiminished, with one falling to Sqn Ldr Tony Lovell, CO of No 145 Sqn, on 16 November after he was scrambled at midday in Spitfire IIB P8533 and intercepted a Ju 88 at 100 ft 25 miles northeast of Hartlepool;

Spitfire VB W3579/OU-Q of No 485 Sqn sits forlornly in the surf near Dunkirk after being hit by flak during a 'Circus' on the afternoon of 31 October. It was being flown by the Kenley Wing Leader, eight-victory ace Wg Cdr Norman Ryder, who became a PoW. Two months earlier the fighter had been used by Flt Lt Stan Norris to achieve his eighth victory (*via Robert Gretzyngier*)

Fighter Command squadrons suffered a steady stream of losses over France throughout 1941, including Spitfire VB W3816/FY-K *The Shopmate* of No 611 Sqn that crash landed after combat with a Bf 109 on 20 September. Its pilot, Battle of Britain ace Flt Lt George Barclay, evaded capture and returned to England via Spain and Gibraltar (*P H T Green Collection*)

'I saw De Wilde striking the engines, cockpit and fuselage and two slight flashes from both engines. Breaking away to port, I looked back and saw that both its engines were blazing fiercely. It went into a shallow dive and exploded on striking the sea.'

Six days later RCAF fighter squadrons had a very successful day during an offensive sweep over the Pas de Calais. They were attacked near St Omer by around 20 Bf 109s and Fw 190s, and in the resulting mêlée No 401 Sqn's Sgt Omer Levesque, who would attain acedom flying F-86s with the US Air Force over Korea, destroyed one of the new Focke-Wulf fighters. Squadronmate and future ace Sgt Don Morrison also claimed his first victory during this action (another Fw 190), and a third Focke-Wulf fell to the CO of No 72 Sqn, Sqn Ldr Cedric Masterman.

The last pilot to become an ace over the Channel Front in 1941 did so on a defensive patrol when, at 1800 ft over the North Sea in mid-afternoon on 17 December, Sqn Ldr Myles Duke-Woolley shot down a Ju 88 to claim No 124 Sqn's first victory, and his fifth overall, as he reported afterwards;

'I fired several short bursts with cannon hoping to prevent enemy aircraft from reaching cover and saw many flashes on its fuselage and port engine. The port engine caught fire and I fired a further burst from 300 yards' range. Three of the crew bailed out in very quick succession, the last one from a height of 200 ft, and his parachute failed to open properly.'

It had been a long, hard year over the Channel for the RAF, with Fighter Command's offensive posture having cost it more than 500 pilots.

A regular task for Fighter Command's Spitfire units in 1941-43 was the escorting of vulnerable Coastal Command aircraft on anti-shipping sweeps. Spitfire VB AD185/QV E of No 19 Sqn is seen on just such a mission on 18 December 1941, when it escorted Beauforts of No 217 Sqn over the North Sea (*R C Nesbit*)

CHAPTER THREE

GREATEST AIR BATTLES

The new year opened with Fighter Command growing stronger, despite sustaining considerable losses. Its main tool remained the Spitfire VB, which could match the Luftwaffe's Bf 109F but was at a considerable disadvantage when pitted against the new Fw 190.

Units in No 11 Group were soon in action, for just after midday on 1 January 1942 Free French ace Flt Lt 'Moses' Demozay of No 91 Sqn was scrambled from Hawkinge after two Bf 109s were detected off Boulogne. He was back before 1300 hrs, having opened Fighter Command's 'book' for 1942. Two hours later, off Le Treport, a trio of Spitfires from No 602 Sqn led by Flg Off Eric Edsall spotted some He 114 reconnaissance seaplanes and shot two of them down. These shared victories made Edsall the first Spitfire pilot to reach acedom in 1942. He was awarded the DFC soon afterwards but subsequently succumbed to wounds suffered during the Japanese raid on Ceylon on 9 April 1942. The first operational Spitfire casualty came the next afternoon when Capt Jens Hertzberg, a Norwegian with No 602 Sqn, ditched on a 'Rhubarb' and was lost.

Gradually, further units continued to receive Spitfires, among them Nos 81 and 134 Sqns after their return from the USSR. On 6 January No 81 Sqn, under Sqn Ldr Tony Rook, began flying convoy escort patrols from Ouston. That same day Flt Lt Jack Ross of No 134 Sqn crashed into the sea near Islay, on the west coast of Scotland, during a convoy escort patrol to become the first ace lost in a Spitfire in 1942. Squadronmate

On 16 January 1942 No 332 Sqn was formed at Catterick as the second Norwegian fighter unit. One of its first aircraft was Spitfire VA R7335/AH-J, which was allocated to future CO Capt Finn Thorshager (*Finn Thorshager via Tor Larsen*)

The first pilot to achieve success in a Spitfire in 1942 was Free French ace Flt Lt Jean-François 'Moses' Demozay, who shot down a Bf 109 off Boulogne at 1230 hrs on 1 January to claim his 15th victory (*via P Hall*)

On returning from the USSR in December 1941, No 134 Sqn was re-equipped with Spitfires. Mk VB AD298/GQ-G was allocated to the CO, Sqn Ldr A G Millar, who subsequently passed it to his successor, Battle of Britain ace Sqn Ldr Keith Lofts (*G A Wilson*)

Flg Off Neil Cameron, a future ace and Chief of the Air Staff, said of his friend, 'His was a great personal loss to me. He was a little man in stature, but very large in spirit and courage'. Another new unit that commenced convoy patrols at this was time was Canadian-manned No 416 Sqn, commanded by Battle of Britain ace Sqn Ldr Paul Webb, which flew its first convoy escorts from Peterhead on 12 January.

Small-scale probing attacks continued, and during one off the Dutch coast on 15 January the Spitfire of Plt Off Tommy Rigler of No 609 Sqn was badly hit by a flakship, wounding him in the shoulder, right arm and leg. He was hospitalised on landing, but soon returned to duty and became an ace during the summer. At the end of the month the second Norwegian fighter unit, No 332 Sqn, was formed at Catterick with Spitfire Vs, joining former Hurricane II unit No 331 Sqn, which had been re-equipped in November 1941. These two exiled units were to produce 14 aces between them over the Channel Front in the next two years.

January ended badly for Fighter Command when Biggin Hill Wing Leader and high-scoring ace Wg Cdr Bob Stanford Tuck did not return from a 'Rhubarb' after his fighter was hit by flak near Boulogne. Force landing on a nearby beach, he soon became a PoW. Gradually, the RAF's core of experienced fighter pilots and leaders was being whittled away.

Early February saw a sustained period of very poor weather, with much ice and snow that precluded any flying in the first ten days of the month. The weather was ideal for the enemy, however. Indeed, the Germans had for some time been planning Operation *Cerberus* – the audacious move of the battlecruisers *Scharnhorst* and *Gneisenau*, along with the heavy cruiser *Prinz Eugen*, from Brest through the English Channel back to Germany. Under a massive Luftwaffe fighter umbrella organised by Oberst Adolf Galland, the operation began when the ships sailed under the mask of heavy weather late on 11 February. The move was not detected until the flotilla was in the Channel the following morning, No 91 Sqn Spitfires on 'Jim Crow' anti-shipping patrols spotting them. Newly appointed squadron CO Sqn Ldr Bobby Oxspring recalled in his autobiography;

'Following the coast past Le Touquet towards the Somme estuary, we suddenly ran into some bursts of heavy flak. Banking into a turn, we peered down through the rain and sighted three much larger ships in line astern, all leaving creamy wakes, indicating the force was moving fast.'

However, their R/T message was not received. The first official confirmation came when Spitfire aces Gp Capt Victor Beamish and Wg Cdr Finlay Boyd from Kenley landed after a patrol. Their report galvanised the first major air action of the year on the Channel Front – Operation *Fuller*. Six Swordfish of 825 Naval Air Squadron, positioned at Manston, launched at 1225 hrs with the promise of strong fighter escort. Poor visibility combined with inept fighter control meant that only the ten aircraft of No 72 Sqn, led by Sqn Ldr Brian Kingcome, actually found the highly vulnerable biplane torpedo-bombers. As the Swordfish headed out at low level, their escorts were given a scant briefing. Kingcome (in AB150/RN-J) had been told, 'Get to Manston [from Gravesend] to escort six Swordfish and intervene between German E-Boats and British MTBs'.

A swarm of enemy fighters soon enveloped the Swordfish, all of which were shot down. In the gloom Plt Off Eric Bocock flew almost overhead the *Gneisenau* as it fired its main armament, before getting onto the tail of an Fw 190 as it chased his No 2. Future ace Bocock easily held the turn and fired a long burst, seeing debris fly off as the Focke-Wulf started to trail black smoke before it fell away into the churning sea. Bocock had claimed his first success.

Having missed the rendevous with No 72 Sqn and the Swordfish, the remaining two units of the Biggin Hill Wing, led by Sqn Ldr Myles Duke-Woolley, eventually engaged the enemy fleet and its fighter escort. Several claims were made, as No 401 Sqn's diarist duly noted;

'Plt Off "Ormie" Ormston nailed a '109, then joined Harley and Sgt Don Morrison and three of them bagged another. Plt Off [J A O] Levesque, followed by Sgt MacDonald, engaged a swarm of Jerries and chased them in and out of France in a mad whirl. Levesque did not return. He will certainly be missed – we feel certain that he brought at least one down.'

The French-Canadian pilot was picked up by the Germans. In contrast, the Hornchurch Wing was ordered to patrol Calais, although by the time it arrived on station the German flotilla had long since passed so units involved saw little action. Gp Capt Victor Beamish's Kenley Wing was tasked with escorting a Beaufort attack, and he strafed a destroyer – 'I raked it from stem to stern. The ship's fire was intense'. Sqn Ldr 'Bluey' Truscott also strafed a ship, whilst the Kiwis of No 485 Sqn were engaged by fighters, as future V1 ace Plt Off Harvey Sweetman described 60 years later;

'The torpedo-bomber unit did not make the rendezvous and No 485 Sqn continued on vector until it suddenly encountered the German fighter protection screen. The weather at the time was poor. Cloud base varied between 500 and 1000 ft, with patches of drizzle. We were fortunate to shoot down three Me 109s without any losses. Bill Compton accounted for one of these aircraft.'

Future Malta ace Flt Sgt Jack Rae also remembered the day in his autobiography;

'Words cannot adequately describe the incredible chaos and sights of raw power, incredible bravery and sheer will to survive that we encountered.

The first major aerial action of the year came on 12 February when the Germans instigated Operation *Cerberus* – the audacious move of the battlecruisers *Scharnhorst* and *Gneisenau*, along with the heavy cruiser *Prinz Eugen*, from Brest through the English Channel back to Germany. The first official confirmation that the operation was underway came from Wg Cdr Victor Beamish, North Weald Wing Leader, who spotted the vessels during a routine patrol over the Channel (*author's collection*)

Whilst flying over the German fleet in poor weather on 12 February future ace Sgt Peter Durnford of No 111 Sqn probably destroyed a Bf 109 to record his first claim (*P Durnford via A Price*)

On 12 February Sgt Peter Durnford was flying Spitfire VB W3848/JU-H painted in the unusual overall black colour scheme worn by No 111 Sqn aircraft at this time due to the unit being assigned nightfighting duties (*P Durnford via A Price*)

I was with Reg Grant. "Hawkeye" [Wells] had led us through the initial break in the clouds, but suddenly there were just the four of us surrounded by masses of the Luftwaffe, who appeared to be even more confused than we were. Reg and I got ourselves involved in a dogfight resulting in Reg destroying an Me 109 which spun into the sea. I didn't wait to see what happened to mine – I knew it had been considerably damaged. All in all it was an unimaginable shambles.'

The day also saw the Debden Wing, led by Gp Capt John Peel, have its first taste of action in 1942, as future ace Sgt Peter Durnford of No 111 Sqn recounted many years later;

'The Wing Commander Flying dashed into the briefing room and said, "The German fleet is coming through the Channel – follow me!" He took off and we followed him. We went out over the sea, and the next thing I knew we had run into a whole lot of '109s. There was a terrific low-level scrap and our squadron was split up. I fired on a '109 and saw strikes around the cockpit – it rolled onto its back and went down. Due to the very low height –100 ft or so – it must have gone in (I was later awarded a "Probable").'

The 21-year-old pilot used W3848/JU-H to make his first claim. Czech squadronmate Plt Off Josef Prihoda (flying R7192/JU-L) was also successful, shooting down a Bf 109. Interestingly, as No 111 Sqn was dedicated to nightfighting duties, its Spitfires were painted black overall and sometimes disparagingly referred to as 'Blackfires'.

No 65 Sqn encountered Bf 109s and Fw 190s 15 miles off Dunkirk, and in the ensuing action Sqn Ldr Humphrey Gilbert destroyed a Messerschmitt to reach acedom. From North Weald, the Canadians of No 403 Sqn were also involved, Flt Sgt Jack Ryckman downing a Bf 109 whilst future ace Plt Off Charles Magwood made his combat debut, recalling 'I saw very little other than my leader's tailwheel!' Elsewhere, from Westhampnett, No 41 Sqn was scrambled at 1350 hrs and encountered 20 Bf 109s five miles off the Belgian coast. In the resulting skirmish three enemy fighters fell, including one to Sqn Ldr 'Dutch' Hugo for the first of his 14 Spitfire victories. In the final Spitfire action of the day No 234 Sqn's Flt Lt Don McKay (in BL241/AZ-E) claimed two Bf 109s destroyed to take his total to 14. North of Dunkirk, he had descended through cloud and spotted three Messerschmitts about 1000 ft below. Closing behind the righthand aircraft, McKay fired a burst from about 200 yards that caused it to pitch up and collide with its leader, resulting in both crashing into the sea.

The so-called 'Channel Dash' was an embarrassment for the Royal Navy and the RAF, with 42 aircraft (ten of which were Spitfires) being lost. However, although a tactical success for the enemy, the threat posed to the Atlantic convoys by the warships based in Brest had now gone.

After the events of the previous day, in which he had played a key part, Gp Capt Victor Beamish was over the Channel once more on 13 February. Encountering a seaplane he thought was an He 114, he quickly shot it down for his first Spitfire victory. Three days later the Czechs of No 312 Sqn achieved their first Spitfire success when Flg Off Otmar Kucera (flying BL381/DU-L), on a convoy patrol off Linney Head, shot down a Ju 88 to also make him the latest Czech ace. Another European exile meeting success was No 609 Sqn's Flg Off Yvan du Monceau de Bergendael, who, in his new Spitfire VB AD396, shot down a Do 217 during a convoy escort on 18 February.

Several days earlier, following a further review, the RAF decided to return to larger-scale operations over the Continent as weather improved. The situation facing Fighter Command in respect to the Spitfire V's inferiority to the Fw 190 had not changed, however, and during a 'Rhubarb' on the 20th No 602 Sqn's new CO, Sqn Ldr 'Paddy' Finucane, was wounded in combat with the increasingly numerous Focke-Wulf. He was hospitalised for two weeks.

More intensive offensive operations resumed in early March thanks to the arrival of better weather, but these inevitably saw an increase in the casualty rate. One of the first to be lost was newly appointed North Weald Wing Leader Wg Cdr Tony Eyre (a Battle of Britain ace), flying with No 121 Sqn. Shot down on 8 March by future 22-victory *experte* Leutnant Artur Beese of 1./JG 26, Eyre became a PoW. During that 'Circus' Flt Lt Cyril Wood of No 403 Sqn shot down a Bf 109F near Gravelines for his sixth claim, of which four were destroyed. Sadly, this promising pilot failed to make ace prior to being killed during a sweep off Dunkirk on the evening of 14 April – he was shot down into the Channel by the *Geschwader Kommodore* of JG 26, Major Gerhard Schöpfel.

Also enjoying success on 8 March was du Monceau de Bergendael, who noted in his log book, 'Off Gravelines about 12 FW 190s sighted. Two different groups of scraps. Miss one. Shoot down another (black and red

The experienced Wg Cdr David Scott-Malden became the North Weald Wing Leader in March 1942, and in that post he made regular claims and became an ace (*via C F Shores*)

Seen in its revetment at North Weald in the late spring of 1942, Spitfire VB AB202/ S-M was the personal mount of Wg Cdr David Scott-Malden. He used it to share in the destruction of two Fw 190s, as well as probably destroying or damaging six more enemy aircraft (*George Aitken*)

smoke). Damage another'. As he headed for home he glanced over his shoulder and saw 'his' Fw 190 splash into the sea just off the beach at Calais. The next day No 452 Sqn claimed its first victories of the year when Sqn Ldr 'Bluey' Truscott downed a Bf 109 and Flt Lt 'Bardie' Wawn claimed two more. The former reported;

'I opened fire on this Me 109E at about 400 yards' range, allowing what I thought to be too much deflection Almost immediately the enemy aircraft rolled over emitting a thick stream of white smoke and went straight down in a side-slipping attitude. I watched the enemy aircraft go down to the ground.'

9 March also saw Sqn Ldr Lloyd Chadburn – soon to become one of the great fighter leaders of the Channel Front – promoted to become No 416 Sqn's first Canadian 'Boss'.

Far to the west, Spitfire VB-equipped No 131 Sqn claimed its first victory when, flying from Valley on 12 March, Flt Lt Ray Harries and Sgt A B F Vilboux shot down a marauding Ju 88 over the Irish Sea. This proved to be the first of Harries' 18 victories. The next day 'Paddy' Finucane returned to action while leading No 602 Sqn as top cover for a 'Circus'. Running in over Hazebrouck at 23,000 ft, he engaged an Fw 190 in a fast running fight. As the Focke-Wulf turned across his nose, his fire took its tail clean off. Pulling around, Finucane closed on another and, in concert with a second pilot, sent the Fw 190 down near the town. One of the RAF's leading aces at that time, the Irishman was asked during an interview about the key to his success;

'The first necessity in combat is to see the other bloke before he sees you – and I've been blessed with a good pair of eyes. The second is to hit him when you fire. You don't get a second chance in this game.'

On 14 March, during an action off Le Havre at 1700 hrs, No 452 Sqn claimed its final victories in the UK (prior to being despatched to Australia) when Sgt Morrison shot down a Bf 109. Appropriately, the unit's last aerial success fell to the leading RAAF ace, Sqn Ldr 'Bluey' Truscott, who described the event as follows;

'The enemy aircraft was an FW 190, and I found little difficulty in holding him in the turn. After about a six- to eight-second burst at close range I could not hold deflection any longer and overshot the FW. I next saw him on my starboard side diving very low towards the coast north of Le Havre. He was emitting a thin trail of black smoke, and when about one mile off the coast I saw him suddenly crash into the sea.'

Sadly, that day at Debden No 111 Sqn lost its CO, Sqn Ldr G F Brotchie, in an accident. He was quickly replaced by Sqn Ldr Peter Wickham, who had become an ace over Libya and Greece. By then its black Spitfires had begun to be repainted in more conventional camouflage, as both Nos 65 and 111 Sqns returned to day fighter duties. Commenting on this change, future ace Sgt Tony Jonsson noted, 'At last our Spits were allowed to discard their "black night gowns" and change back to their ordinary day clothes. With this our spirits rose anew'.

Another new CO was Sqn Ldr Wilf Duncan-Smith in No 64 Sqn, whilst reinforcement for Fighter Command came when Norwegian-manned No 332 Sqn was declared operational at Catterick. The Australians of No 457 Sqn, under the leadership of Hurricane ace Sqn Ldr Peter Brothers, were also deemed ready for action when posted to Redhill, in No 11 Group, in March. Brothers noted some years later, 'We were predominantly flying bomber escorts and fighter sweeps in our Mk VBs, participating in sorties with the Kenley, Hornchurch and Biggin Hill Wings – we often flew top cover for the latter outfit'. No 457 Sqn flew its first 'Circus' operation on the 26th, during which Brothers (flying BM143/BP-A) shot down a Bf 109 to claim the unit's first victory and his 13th. No 485 Sqn was also involved in the action that day, with future high-scoring aces Flt Lt Bill Crawford-Compton and Plt Off Evan Mackie each enjoying success. The former downed a Bf 109 off Le Havre, and moments later he shared a second victory with Mackie (flying AB310/OU-Q). The latter made a head-on attack that was described to a journalist by Crawford-Compton;

'I saw them firing like blazes at each other, and then saw glycol streaming from the Hun after they had passed each other, so I gave the Hun a few seconds' burst. He went down in flames and crashed into the sea a quarter of a mile from the French coast.'

Gp Capt Victor Beamish also shot down a Bf 109E and an Fw 190 that same day to take his total to ten, although two days later his Spitfire was seen to be hit during an engagement with JG 26 and he disappeared into cloud near Calais. The charismatic Station Commander was never seen again, his being one of eight Spitfires lost on 28 March. Another high-scoring ace was lost on 10 April when Tangmere Wing Leader Wg Cdr Michael Robinson (in W3770/MLR) failed to return from a sweep over Boulogne. His wingman, Lt Maurice Choron of No 340 Sqn, was also downed. Battle of Britain ace Robinson left behind an important legacy, as it was at this time that the Tangmere Wing adopted the Luftwaffe-style line abreast formation, as Plt Off Teddy Hall recounted;

'In the new formation losses dropped immediately. Our squadrons could now turn much quicker to face the diving Germans, and we were not taken by surprise as often.'

Hurricane ace Sqn Ldr Peter Brothers helped form No 457 Sqn RAAF in June 1941 and eventually led the unit on its first 'Circus' operation on 26 March 1942. Flying Spitfire VB BM143/BP-A, in which he is seen here, Brothers shot down a Bf 109 over Le Havre to claim the unit's first victory, and his 13th of 16 (*via John Dibbs*)

Plt Off Evan Mackie, who joined No 485 Sqn in early 1942, claimed the first of his 23 victories over France on 26 March. His personal marking reflected his nickname of 'Rosie' (*E D Mackie*)

Czech ace Plt Off Vaclav Jicha of No 313 Sqn ruefully examines the damage to Spitfire VB BM306/RY-E after it was attacked by an Fw 190 over Lille on 5 May 1942. A few days earlier he had damaged a Focke-Wulf in this aircraft to record his final claim (*Jiri Rajlich*)

Nevertheless, before April was out the new Tangmere Wing Leader, Wg Cdr 'Dutch' Hugo, had also been lost in combat with Fw 190s off Dover on the 27th, although he bailed out wounded and was rescued. It was not a good day for Fighter Command, which lost 17 Spitfires, with ten pilots killed or missing, two wounded and four becoming PoWs. This was a clear indication of how intense the action was becoming as the spring progressed, as is the example of Plt Off Gray Stenborg of No 111 Sqn. He began his path to acedom when, over the Pas de Calais near Mont Cassel, he shot down an Fw 190 on the 26th. The young New Zealander then shot down three more fighters over the next four days, before becoming an ace after being posted to Malta.

NEW MARKS

To improve the Spitfire's high-altitude performance, the Mk VI was developed from the Mk V through the fitment of a Merlin 47 engine driving a four-bladed propeller, extended wingtips and a pressurised cockpit. The first examples entered service with No 616 Sqn, led by Sqn Ldr Harry Broun (who had claimed several victories flying Gladiator IIs with No 112 Sqn in Greece the previous year), in April 1942. Flying its first operational sortie on 9 May, the Spitfire VI was developed primarily to counter the very high-flying Luftwaffe reconnaissance aircraft that had previously criss-crossed the UK with impunity. The new Spitfire (only 100 of which were built) proved unpopular with pilots, however, principally because of its clamped cockpit hood that could not be opened in flight.

Early May also saw the establishment of the Czech Wing comprising Nos 310 and 312 Sqns under the command of experienced ace Wg Cdr Alois Vasatko. On the 17th No 310 Sqn flew a sweep that was engaged by Fw 190s, as its CO, Sqn Ldr Karel Mrazek, recalled;

'I had heard some hair-raising tales about them, but had reserved my judgment. In no time flat I came to the conclusion that everything that I had heard was true, but I never lost confidence in my Spitfire as a fighting lady. It had been an eye-opener.'

Also successful that day was Hornchurch Wing Leader Wg Cdr

Peter Powell, who destroyed an Fw 190 over Audruicq for his last victory. However, by the beginning of June losses had reached unsustainable proportions, and operations were temporarily suspended over the Continent following a 'Circus' to Belgium on the 1st that had seen Spitfires from the Hornchurch, Debden and Biggin Hill Wings attacked out of the sun by more than 40 Fw 190s of I. and III./JG 26. Led by the redoubtable Hauptmann 'Pips' Priller, the German pilots shot down ten Spitfires, including that of Debden Wing Leader Wg Cdr J A G Gordon, who went down near Bruges. One pilot who claimed a victory in return was Flt Lt Yvan du Monceau de Bergendael, now flying with his Belgian countrymen in No 350 Sqn. He shot down an Fw 190 off Nieuport to become an ace.

There were further losses the next day when, during a 'Rodeo' by the North Weald Wing led by Wg Cdr David Scott-Malden, the inexperienced No 403 Sqn under Sqn Ldr Al Deere was trapped at 27,000 ft by Fw 190s during the withdrawal and seven of its Spitfires were shot down. Amongst the pilots killed was Battle of Britain ace Flt Lt 'Mitzi' Darling. Earlier that same day the Hornchurch Wing, led by Wg Cdr Peter Powell, lost six more Spitfires and their pilots, whilst Powell (flying BM308/PP) was wounded in the head by shell splinters – he suffered a fracture at the base of the skull. Sqn Ldr Wilf Duncan-Smith shepherded him home;

'I could see that he was in distress and not sure where he was. His canopy had gone and a large hole behind the cockpit area stared at me bleakly.'

On a more positive note, 2 June saw No 81 Sqn claim its first victories since the unit's sojourn in Murmansk when, off Le Touquet, future ace Flt Lt James Walker (in BM315) shot down an Fw 190 and Flt Lt Bedford got another. The next day Canadian Flt Sgt John Portz, who would make 11 claims, including four destroyed, was credited with one of No 242 Sqn's very few Spitfire successes in the UK when, in scattered cloud 60 miles off Fife Ness, he probably destroyed a Ju 88.

Despite the recent losses some Wing sweeps continued. On 5 June, for example, the trio of units forming the Biggin Hill Wing headed for France, No 91 Sqn, whose CO Sqn Ldr Bobby Oxspring flew as wingman to the Leader, Wg Cdr Jamie Rankin, leading the way, with Sqn Ldr Brian Kingcome's No 72 Sqn above them and No 124 Sqn, led by Sqn Ldr Myles Duke-Woolley, as top cover. Oxspring described Jamie Rankin's 23rd, and final victory, scored during the course of this mission;

One of the many 'exiled European' squadrons was the Belgian-manned No 350 Sqn, to which Spitfire VB BL540/MN-Y belonged. It was flown by Flt Lt Yvan de Monceau de Bergendael who claimed two Fw 190s damaged with it during May. He was also at the fighter's controls when he shot down a Focke-Wulf on 1 June to achieve acedom (*Count Y de Monceau de Bergendael via P Celis*)

Flt Lt Count Yvan de Monceau de Bergendael in the cockpit of BL540 after his fifth victory. He was one of the most successful Belgian pilots of the war (*Count Y de Monceau de Bergendael via P Celis*)

Spitfire VB BM124/LO-W was a presentation aircraft from the people of Tonga, being named after the island nation's long-reigning monarch Queen Salote. It also wore the shamrock marking of its pilot, No 602 Sqn CO Sqn Ldr 'Paddy' Finucane, who, through the spring of 1942, achieved four victories, four probables and four damaged in it. Although lacking its pilot's burgeoning scoreboard, BM124 was adorned with No 602 Sqn's lion marking as well as a bottle of champagne! (*via Dugald Cameron*)

'Over Abbeville a gaggle of Me 109s fell on us out of the sun, but not before we saw them. 124 Squadron turned into them and engaged as 72 Squadron cut across to help. At the same time Jamie winged over, calling a sighting beneath us. As I followed him down I saw a string of Focke-Wulf 190s climbing up in ones and twos, and way below more pairs taking off from an airfield. Jamie snaked down behind a '190 and let fly from close range – a cluster of shells from his cannons flashed into the fuselage around the cockpit area. Flame and smoke shot back as his victim fell into its fatal dive. Without pause Jamie moved over and belted another '190 as it struggled for altitude. Pieces of cowling and the canopy peeled off, followed by the pilot, who hastily departed on his parachute. Lost in admiration at this awesome display of shooting, I almost forgot my primary duty to guard our tails.'

On 21 June 'Paddy' Finucane was promoted to Wing Commander and appointed as the Hornchurch Wing Leader – at 21, he was the youngest in the RAF! Also promoted to lead the Ibsley Wing was 'Bunny' Currant from No 501 Sqn, who, by comparison, was an 'old man' of 30. By the end of the month their colleague at North Weald, Wg Cdr David Scott-Malden, had joined them in the pantheon of aces when, on the 29th, he shared an Fw 190 during a 'Circus'. Five pilots were lost from Nos 222 and 331 Sqns during this mission, however, including the CO of 'Treble Two', Sqn Ldr Newton Anderson. On the last day of the month the Norwegian unit finally opened its Spitfire account when Lt Stein Sem and future ace Lt Fredrik Fearnley shared a Bf 109 destroyed off Flushing.

By then the RAF had been presented with an unexpected and extremely welcome gift from the Luftwaffe. On 23 June the Czech Wing, led by Wg Cdr Alois Vasatko, escorted Bostons against Morlaix airfield. During the course of the mission Plt Off Josef Prihoda of No 313 Sqn hit an Fw 190 that dived vertically into the sea for his final victory. Focke-Wulfs then continually harried the withdrawing force across the Channel, with Unteroffizier Wilhelm Reushling actually colliding with the Czech Wing Leader, who was lost, although the German pilot bailed out and was picked up off Brixham. Oberleutnant Armin Faber of 7./JG 2, having shot down a Spitfire of No 310 Sqn, became disoriented after being separated from his unit during the mêlée and headed north. He eventually landed at Pembrey, thus presenting the RAF with an undamaged example of the Fw 190. Comparative trials with the Spitfire V quickly confirmed its qualities, although the Mk IX that was then entering service was generally considered to be its equal.

A large amphibious raid on the port of Dieppe, known as Operation *Rutter*, had been planned for early July, but this was postponed due to bad weather. Preparatory activity and 'routine' offensive missions continued, nevertheless. However, on the 15th, nine Spitfires were lost on a 'Rhubarb', or the subsequent air-sea rescue (ASR) cover. One of those posted missing was Hornchurch Wing Leader Wg Cdr 'Paddy' Finucane, who was hit by ground fire and then ditched in the Channel. His demise was witnessed by future ace Plt Off Alan Aikman;

'He jettisoned the cockpit canopy. It was a textbook ditching, but the Spitfire suddenly disappeared in a wall of water – it nosed down and sank instantly. There was no sign of Finucane.'

It was a huge loss – he had claimed 30 victories since the start of 1941, and was to remain the most successful ace over the Channel Front. Three days later, during a convoy patrol, No 416 Sqn opened its account when Flt Lt Phil Archer shot down a Do 217 in overcast weather just east of Orfordness, this victory also making him an ace.

The Spitfire VI had been 'blooded' on 13 July when No 616 Sqn's Flt Lt Tony Gaze had claimed an Fw 190 probable. Five days later, west of Le Touquet, he claimed the type's first confirmed victory that also made the Australian an ace. His victim was an Fw 190 of 5./JG 26, destroyed, ironically, at low level, as he described;

'I turned and chased them using 14 lb of boost and managed to close in to 500 yards. I dived steeply to sea level and managed to get ahead of them, 500 ft below the leader, and pulled up underneath him, firing a short burst of cannon and machine gun, which hit him in the belly and starboard wing. His undercarriage dropped and I gave him another burst as he turned left, diving towards the sea. I took a cine shot of the pilot of the first FW who had pulled up in front of me earlier in the fight and bailed

For the original attack on Dieppe, codenamed Operation *Rutter*, participating aircraft received identification stripes as displayed on Spitfire VB BM579/FN-B of No 331 Sqn. This aeroplane was the usual mount of future ace Lt Rolfe Berg, who, over Dieppe on 19 August, shot down an Fw 190 and damaged two more in it before being hit and forced to bail out (*via Tor Larsen*)

out at about 700 ft. As he bailed out flames poured out of the cockpit and the aircraft went straight into the sea.'

Gaze had used 117 cannon rounds and more than 1000 0.303-in bullets. His port cannon stopped after just 25 rounds. Within a week Sqn Ldr Tommy Balmforth's No 124 Sqn had also re-equipped with the Mk VI (only two frontline units would fly the aircraft), performing its first sweep to Fecamp, led by the CO, on the 29th. It patrolled at 19,000 ft without incident. More significantly, that day the RAF's 'stop-gap' answer to the Fw 190, the Spitfire IX, also entered service when Hornchurch-based No 64 Sqn, under Sqn Ldr Duncan-Smith, was declared operational and flew a sweep with Nos 81, 122 and 154 Sqns.

The Spitfire IX was a marriage of the powerful Merlin 61 (and later Merlin 63) engine with the Mk V airframe, thus retaining the older variant's superb handling but greatly improving the fighter's overall performance. Although introduced as a stop-gap, the Spitfire IX became Fighter Command's standard aircraft for the rest of the war. The new Mk IX was soon blooded when, shortly after midday on 30 July, an Fw 190 was destroyed by Flt Lt Don Kingaby (flying BR600) west of Boulogne, his victim possibly being Oberleutnant Herbert Heck, who crashed on the coast near Samer in Wk-Nr 5303. During a sortie in the evening four more fighters were claimed over St Omer, with Duncan-Smith getting one and sharing a second with future ace Lt Arne Austeen – this was the Norwegian's first success. Duncan-Smith wrote;

'I led the Squadron down again in much the same way as in the morning show, and got a '190 from slightly above and dead astern. No doubt this time – he burst into flames, spiralling down in a cloud of smoke. We got separated as a result of the engagement, so Arne Austeen, my No 2, a Norwegian, and I flew home on our own. A few miles off Calais we found an FW 190 attacking a Spitfire, and since we had plenty of height we went after him. We caught him easily, each attacking in turn and sending the enemy into the sea in flames.'

Rhodesian Plt Off Jim Stewart got a third, with the fourth becoming Belgian Plt Off Michel Donnet's first victory. Also involved was Wg Cdr Don Finlay, the Hornchurch Wing Leader, and ace, flying a Spitfire IX as well. He damaged an Fw 190 to record his final claim. Significantly, Donnet observed, 'The action gave us complete confidence in the Mk IX. Now we felt we were one up on the Focke-Wulf 190s'. Soon after midday on the 30th No 332 Sqn broke its duck when Sgt Marius Eriksen claimed the first of his nine victories;

'As I crossed the French coast south of Le Touquet I saw two FW 190s going south at zero feet. I went after the last one and gave him a three-second burst from 300-350 yards, but had to remain out to sea owing to the heavy flak from the shore. I looked for the FW 190 and saw smoke coming from his engine, then I saw him land with wheels up

The RAF's answer to the Fw 190 was the Spitfire IX, and amongst the first examples to reach the frontline was this aeroplane delivered to No 64 Sqn in July 1942. The Mk IX was the Focke-Wulf's equal in most respects, and it duly became the RAF's standard fighter in Europe
(P H T Green Collection)

at full speed on the sand just north of Berck, bouncing several times before taking a header into the sea.'

Within days Canadian-manned No 401 Sqn was re-equipped with the Spitfire IX, commencing operations from Biggin Hill on 3 August. Two days later No 611 Sqn flew its first Mk IX operation, covering the USAF's 308th Fighter Squadron (FS) on a sweep over Le Touquet. Both RAF units achieved their first Spitfire IX victories on the 17th, as did No 402 Sqn from Kenley (which had begun Mk IX operations four days earlier) when escorting USAAF B-17s of the 97th Bomb Group (BG) on a raid on railway marshalling yards at Rouen. They continued escorting Flying Fortresses on some of their early missions, which marked a significant change in the air war over Europe.

The CO of No 111 Sqn, desert ace Sqn Ldr Peter Wickham, stands in front of Spitfire VB EP166/JU-N. He flew this aeroplane on five sorties over Dieppe on 19 August, during which he damaged two Bf 109s. It carries No 111 Sqn's pre-war black bar marking just above the wing root (No 111 Sqn Records)

DUELS OVER DIEPPE

The delayed raid on Dieppe, now codenamed Operation *Jubilee*, was rescheduled for 19 August, and it was to result in perhaps the greatest aerial battle fought over Western Europe in World War 2. For the raid, fighter squadrons of Nos 10, 11 and 12 Groups were concentrated on airfields along the south coast to ensure complete cover over both Dieppe itself and the assault shipping involved in the operation during daylight hours. As well as the four units flying the new Mk IX and two with the Mk VI, the force included no fewer than 42 squadrons flying the Spitfire V.

Well before dawn, as the landing force edged towards the coast, the first elements providing the top cover prepared to take off. At West Malling, for example, No 610 Sqn was at readiness by 0300 hrs. First off at 0415 hrs was No 111 Sqn from Kenley, led by Sqn Ldr Peter Wickham in EP166/JU-N, followed five minutes later by Sqn Ldr Desmond McMullen's No 65 Sqn from Eastchurch. Both units were tasked with covering Blenheims laying a smoke screen to blind enemy coastal batteries. They arrived over Dieppe at 0440 hrs, No 111 Sqn's pilots subsequently noting that the stars were still shining. They were the first of a stream of fighters that covered the area throughout the day, Wickham, for example, flying five sorties on the 19th – two leading his own unit and three at the head of the inexperienced 308th FS. During the course of these missions he damaged two Fw 190s.

Other fighter units were tasked with attacking gun emplacements, and on one such sortie Flg Off Harry Jones' No 129 Sqn aircraft became the first Spitfire lost. On the way back his wingman, Sgt Reeves, had the Spitfire's first brush with the Luftwaffe.

As Nos 65 and 111 Sqns departed, No 124 Sqn's Spitfire VIs, in company with No 71 'Eagle' Sqn led by Wg Cdr Myles Duke-Woolley, were over the ships, being joined by 'Dutch' Hugo's Hornchurch Wing (Nos 81, 122, 154 and 340 Sqns). As the scale of the assault became evident, the Luftwaffe began appearing in greater numbers, although this initial group had only inconclusive brushes with the enemy. Four Polish squadrons relieved the group, and they were in turn replaced by Nos 402, 602 and 611 Sqns as the sun rose above the horizon. Again, there were several skirmishes.

And so the long day started. The Tangmere Wing arrived over the town soon after 0600 hrs to cover a Boston attack, whilst also up was Sqn Ldr Douglas Watkins' No 611 Sqn. He recalled;

'At 0610 hrs a Fw 190 dived down to my height (1500 ft) and swept round behind my No 2. I throttled back and easily turned inside the enemy aircraft and fired a short burst at 45 degrees' deflection – I saw one cannon strike behind the cockpit of the enemy aircraft and he flew straight inland over the River Bethune at 100 ft. The enemy aircraft apparently tried to make a forced landing on the high ground southwest of the river mouth and hit the ground, bouncing into the air in a cloud of dust.'

The first victory of the day also took Watkins to acedom.

By the time Wg Cdr David Scott-Malden's North Weald Wing, comprising No 242 Sqn led by 1940 ace Sqn Ldr Tom Parker and the Norwegians of Nos 331 and 332 Sqn as top cover, appeared over the ships shortly before 0700 hrs, the Luftwaffe had committed significantly more aircraft to the defence of Dieppe. No 332 Sqn soon became embroiled in a terrific dogfight, losing two Spitfires but shooting down three Focke-Wulfs in return. Sgt Marius Eriksen got one of them;

After achieving his first success over Dieppe, Lt Rolf Arne Berg went on to become a distinguished Wing Leader until his death in combat on 3 February 1945 (*via Tor Larsen*)

'Just off coast, we were attacked by FW 190s. I managed to get on the tail of one of the four FW 190s that were trying to get into position for attack on one of our Spitfires. I gave him a burst and observed hits. The FW 190 turned on its back but the enemy aircraft then turned back into level position, giving me an opportunity to close in on it from rear. I gave him two to three bursts, observing hits all the time. The enemy aircraft again turned on its back and dived down with smoke pouring out of the engine. He did not pull out of this dive and he hit the sea with a huge splash.'

However, his CO, Maj Wilhelm Mohr, who, post-war became head of the Royal Norwegian Air Force, was wounded by an Fw 190, whilst Sgt Per Bergsland was shot down. He later took part in the 'Great Escape', making it to freedom. No 331 Sqn also enjoyed success, with its CO, Maj Helge Mehre, claiming the second of his six victories;

'I remember that first clash with the Luftwaffe in the morning. During the dogfight my No 2 was hit by an FW 190 and had to bail out. I managed to turn in behind the '190s and closed on the rear one. I put a good four- to five-second burst into him. He emitted black smoke and the pilot jumped out of his aircraft, which then turned over into a vertical dive.'

Fellow future ace and outstanding leader Capt Kaj Birksted also claimed his second victory in this action. With 12.5 confirmed between them, the two Norwegian squadrons were the most successful of the day. Another European exile unit in action was Belgian-manned No 350 Sqn, with Flt Lt Yvan du Monceau de Bergendael (flying EN794/MN-X on this first mission) shooting down an Fw 190, as he noted in his flying log book. 'Attack with Blue section some FW 190s. One goes down spinning and in flames off Dieppe after one-second burst'. Other pilots from the unit shared a second Fw 190.

Fighter cover continued from the West Malling Wing, in which No 610 Sqn was led by Sqn Ldr 'Johnnie' Johnson. When the unit was attacked by 50 enemy fighters, Johnson sent an Fw 190 crashing into the sea, before sharing in the destruction of a Bf 109 – his first victories of the year. During this intense dogfight his colleague Flt Lt Denis Crowley-Milling (flying EP361/DW-H) attacked a Bf 109 on the tail of a Spitfire. His first burst found its mark, flipping the Messerschmitt over and leaving it streaming glycol. The pilot soon bailed out.

Thirty miles from Dieppe was the major fighter airfield at Abbeville, against which an attack by 24 B-17s of the 97th BG was planned for mid-morning. Four squadrons of Spitfire IXs escorted them, and as bombs rained onto the airfield at least 12 fighters were seen to take off. When the Fw 190s attacked as the force departed, recently promoted Plt Off Don Morrison of No 401 Sqn engaged one of the enemy aeroplanes. He later recalled the action for the RCAF Official History;

'I saw a single FW 190 just ahead and about 1500 ft below me. I did a slipping barrel roll, losing height and levelling out about 150 yards behind and slightly to starboard and above the enemy aircraft. I opened fire with a two-second burst, closing to 25 yards. I saw strikes all along the starboard side of the fuselage, and several pieces that seemed about a foot square flew off from around the cowling. Just as both the enemy aircraft and myself ran into cloud, he exploded with a terrific flash of flame and black smoke. Immediately after this my windshield and hood were covered with oil and there was a terrific clatter as pieces of debris struck my aircraft. I broke away, hardly able to see through my hood or windshield. My No 2 said he saw a piece about ten feet long break off the enemy aircraft.'

The dramatic action had taken Morrison to acedom, but damage from the debris forced him to bail out. He was picked up by a boat and then suffered the trauma of being attacked by enemy aircraft whilst at sea, during which he leaped overboard to save a badly wounded man from a stricken launch.

Plt Off Don Morrison of No 401 Sqn was one of the leading RCAF pilots from late 1941 until he was shot down on 8 November 1942. Badly wounded in the legs by a cannon shell, Morrison had to have one of them amputated by German surgeons (*Canadian Forces*)

The aerial action was to continue for much of the day, with the troop withdrawal commencing at 1100 hrs. Above Dieppe at this time, No 124 Sqn's Spitfire VIs saw considerable combat that resulted in victories for Plt Offs Johnnie Hull and Mike Kilburn, both future aces. Flt Sgt Peter Durnford attacked another Fw 190 from 200 yards, and after his second burst he saw the fighter erupt in flames – the aeroplane was later confirmed as destroyed. Then he spotted a bomber below him;

'I saw a Ju 88 flying at 2000 ft. As I dived to within 300 yards of the enemy aircraft it immediately descended to tree-top level. I closed the range to about 250 yards and gave a one-second burst, seeing strikes around the port engine nacelle. After I had fired the remainder of my cannons the enemy aircraft dropped its bombs. I immediately did a steep climbing turn to the right to about 2000 ft and, looking down, saw the Ju 88 crash into a field with a dark smoke trail coming from its port engine, which had stopped.'

Upon Durnford's return to base his camera gun showed his victim to have been a Do 217.

The battles over the coast and the remnants of the invasion flotillas as they withdrew continued through the afternoon, resulting in a steady stream of losses and claims. An Fw 190 fell in the early afternoon to Plt Off 'Sammy' Sampson of No 602 Sqn, who, shortly before 1400 hrs, had found himself off Dieppe at 10,000 ft;

'Two FW 190s appeared no more than 100 yards in front of us, climbing away from the ships and crossing away to our left. I don't think the Hun pilot saw me, for he turned to starboard, which allowed me to give him a three-second burst from 150 yards. He went down on fire into the sea, very close to our ships.'

Squadronmate Flt Lt Eric Bocock claimed a Do 217 destroyed (and an Fw 190 damaged) to become an ace. The Norwegians were active again throughout the afternoon, with 2/Lt Svein Heglund claiming his first victory – by war's end he would be Norway's ranking ace. Lt Rolfe Berg also set out on the path to acedom, although he was forced to bail out of BL579/FN-B after being attacked by an Fw 190. Berg was rescued by the launch ML190 and landed at Newhaven.

Mid-afternoon, the Tangmere Wing, led by Wg Cdr Pat Gibbs (in EP120/SD-Y), flew out to escort the homeward-bound vessels carrying the troops that had been evacuated. The ships were being constantly harassed

No 118 Sqn's Sgt Tommy de Courcey used Spitfire VB EP130/NK-Y to share in the destruction of a Do 217 with Wg Cdr Pat Gibbs over Dieppe on 19 August. De Courcey would make six aerial and two strafing claims in Spitfires between 1942 and 1945 (*Clive Anderton*)

by German bombers, resulting in several contacts between Spitfires from the Wing and Do 217s and Fw 190s. Gibbs spotted three Dorniers as they broke cloud and chased one of them, opening fire at a range of 500 yards and seeing many hits as the bomber suddenly lost speed when one of its engines seized. He then turned to counter an attack from Fw 190s as Sgt Tommy de Courcey from No 118 Sqn (in EP130/NK-Y) finished off the crippled bomber. Another Do 217 fell to future ace Flt Lt John Shepherd, also from No 118 Sqn. Action continued into the evening, with one of the last engagements involving Sqn Ldr Michael Pedley's No 131 Sqn – he shared in the downing of a Ju 88.

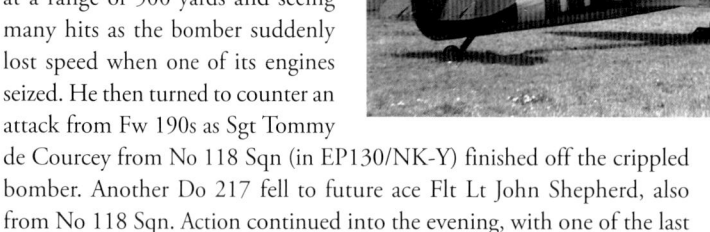

In one of the greatest aerial battles of World War 2, 62 Spitfires and 29 pilots had been lost. Sqn Ldr 'Johnnie' Johnson, later the most successful Spitfire pilot of the war, concluded, 'Our Spitfire Vs were completely outclassed by the FW 190s, and on this occasion I was certainly lucky to get back'.

There was little respite for Fighter Command after the intense action of Dieppe. For example, during the afternoon of 24 August, 12 B-17s attacked the Le Trait shipyards in Normandy. The escort for the missions included Spitfire IXs from No 611 Sqn, which maintained an altitude of 31,000 ft above the bombers. During the mission Flt Lt Vernon Crawford-Compton claimed his seventh victory;

'I was flying at 26,000 ft behind the beehive on the way out from the bombing of Le Trait. When flying west of Fauville I saw three Fw 190s below me and climbing up to the bombers. I turned behind them and came up underneath the port '190. I started firing at about 300 yards and kept on until I had to break away and flames appeared underneath the front cowling and spread along the fuselage.'

Although he then broke away to counter other attacks, his victory was confirmed, as was the Fw 190 attacked by No 402 Sqn's CO, Sqn Ldr Bretz.

No 124 Sqn's high-altitude Spitfire VIs also had some success at the end of the month, bringing down two Focke-Wulfs during a 'Circus', one of which fell to Plt Off 'Slim' Kilburn on 29 August for his fourth success. However, the skies over the Pas de Calais continued to be dangerous, and during a sweep on 5 September four Spitfires from No 340 Sqn were shot down by Fw 190s of JG 26. One was BL803/GW-L flown by Cne François de Labouchère (three and one shared victories), who was killed. The following day a B-17 raid escorted by four Spitfire IX squadrons was intercepted by Fw 190s, and in the resulting mêlée Hauptmann Karl-Heinz Meyer of II./JG 26 shot down B-17F 41-24445 *Six Bits* of the 97th BG near Amiens. This was the first US *'Viermot'* to fall to the Luftwaffe, and another bomber was lost a few minutes later.

It was during an escort for B-17s to Morlaix on 26 September by Nos 64 and 401 Sqns and No 133 'Eagle' Sqn that particularly strong winds at high altitude caused the escorting fighters to miss their rendezvous and fly

Portreath Wing Leader Wg Cdr 'Mindy' Blake shot down an Fw 190 in Spitfire VB W3561/MB over Dieppe on 19 August, although he too was forced to bail out shortly thereafter when the aeroplane was hit by fire from another Focke-Wulf. Minden Blake was eventually picked up by a German launch the following morning just five miles off Dover (*via N L R Franks*)

In achieving 3.5 victories in the Spitfire VI with No 124 Sqn, Flt Lt Mike Kilburn was the most successful pilot to fly the high-altitude variant (*via P Listemann*)

further south than planned. Although most landed safely back in England, albeit very short of fuel, the 'Eagle' squadron lost no fewer than 12 Spitfire IXs and 11 pilots.

October saw an improvement in the weather on the previous ten days, and during the afternoon of the 2nd No 611 Sqn was led by Wg Cdr Eric Thomas on a 'Circus' escorting B-17s sent to bomb the aircraft factory at Meaulte. During the return leg of the mission the formation was attacked, and the new CO, Australian Sqn Ldr Hugo 'Sinker' Armstrong, went after a Bf 109 east of Abbeville and probably destroyed it. Wg Cdr Thomas led his Biggin Wing on another mission on the morning of the 9th when he destroyed an Fw 190 near Gravelines to become an ace;

'I was leading the Wing, with 610 Sqn as rear support for Fortresses bombing Lille. I got in a full quarter attack on the leader, which turned out to be a FW 190, and gave a second's burst full deflection from 200 yards and a quick squirt at the other FW 190, which I am sure I missed. The first one went vertically down, followed by his No 2, and I last saw him at about 15,000 ft still going vertically at a phenomenal speed. I had to pull up and around then, but I understand another member of the Squadron saw him crash just off Gravelines in the sea.'

Thomas was then embroiled with more fighters, and after the mission he wrote in his report, 'I claim 1 FW 190 destroyed, 1 FW 190 damaged and 4 FW 190s frightened!'

On 11 October, in clear weather, No 122 Sqn's Sgt Graham 'Ginger' Hulse, flying a Spitfire IX, made his first claim when he damaged an Fw 190 near St Omer;

'I picked up an FW, and getting astern, quickly overhauled him. I opened fire with a one-second mixed burst at 100 yards, but I was going so quickly that I had to cease fire in order to avoid ramming him. I saw strikes on the port trailing edge and engine cowling.'

Hulse was to be credited with 11 claims, including three MiG-15s destroyed, before his loss over Korea in March 1953.

JABO HUNTING

At the end of the month all of I *Gruppe* and part of II *Gruppe* JG 26 were ordered to fit their Fw 190A 4s with bomb racks so as to intensify attacks on England in response to the increasingly heavy attacks by Bomber Command on Germany. They were to supplement the two existing *Jabostaffeln* for a daylight '*Vergeltungsangriff* (vengeance attack) against Canterbury by 49 fighter-bombers and 62 escorts in what would prove to be the biggest daylight attack mounted against England since the autumn of 1940. The force swept across the Channel during the late afternoon of 31 October, achieving complete surprise. Spitfires of Sqn Ldr 'Moses' Demozay's Hawkinge-based No 91 Sqn were scrambled, the CO subsequently recalling;

'I saw four FW 190s slightly below, flying line astern in pairs. I came down and attacked the No 2 of the port pair from astern. All four climbed into cloud and I followed, giving the same enemy aircraft another burst from 300 yards. It went down vertically with thick smoke issuing, and I followed and saw flames issuing from the wing root of the fuselage at

1000 ft. I saw an oil patch and later the Coastguards at Dover reported that an aircraft had been seen to go into the sea at the same time and in the same position.'

Demozay landed to refuel and rearm, before taking off once again;

'Crossing the coast at Folkestone at 300 ft, I saw four more FW 190s flying north at sea level. I fired at the leader of one pair from 200 yards and saw hits on the port side of the engine cowling. I then turned towards the other pair. I chased these two towards Dover, firing short bursts at the No 2 from astern. Ten miles east of Dover the enemy aircraft went straight into the sea.'

This was Demozay's 18th victory, making him one of the leading French aces of the war. His first victim that day may have been Leutnant Paul Galland, *Staffelkapitän* of 8./JG 26, who was lost in Fw 190 Wk-Nr 2402 'Black 1'. Another Focke-Wulf was claimed near Deal by No 122 Sqn's Plt Off Don Mercer, who had been scrambled with the unit from Hornchurch. Recently reformed No 453 Sqn RAAF also had its first brush with the Luftwaffe off Deal that day when its pilots damaged three Fw 190s and a Ju 88, albeit for the loss of Flg Off G G Galwey, who was picked up after a long night paddling his dinghy in the direction of the Kent coast.

Despite deteriorating weather, on 2 November the Biggin Hill Wing mounted a 'Rodeo'. Off the French coast No 611 Sqn's six-victory ace Flg Off David Fulford, who was seen to be lagging behind, crashed into the sea after possibly being bounced by an Fw 190. Shortly thereafter the rest of the unit engaged more Focke-Wulfs, and in the ensuing dogfight Sqn Ldr Armstrong and Flt Lt de Tedesco each destroyed one. Armstrong said of his ninth victory;

'I was able to get to very close range from slightly below before firing. There were strikes all over the belly and around the cockpit, and the enemy aircraft climbed very steeply to port and the pilot baled out as the aircraft stalled and fell down.'

No 340 Sqn was also involved in this mission, its CO, Cdt Bernard Duperier, noting in his combat report;

'I saw two FW.190 climbing below a cloud layer approximately 3000 ft below the Wing. I dived through this cloud layer. Coming out of the cloud I saw in front of me three FW.190s – one at approximately 150-200 yds travelling fast in the same direction, and almost in my reflector sight. I gave a short burst at the first one, from which a large piece immediately flew away – probably a jettisonable hood – and the pilot came out, with his white parachute opening. At this time the other two enemy aircraft in front began to dive towards le Touquet. I gave a long burst at the nearest one, which was approximately 600-800 yds ahead, and a very long trail of blue-grayish smoke came out of the machine, which dived steeply towards the ground.

'I then received a warning telling me that there were some more FW.190s, and I took violent evasive action, during which time I lost sight of the smoking FW.190 for a few seconds, but later I saw in the same area, a few miles south of le Touquet aerodrome, an aircraft crashing to the ground with a large explosion.'

The two Fw 190s Duperier destroyed made him the latest Free French ace. Adj Robert Gouby was also successful, and the Fw 190 that he was credited with was his first step to acedom. The French unit was in

With a pressurised cockpit, improved engine and extended wingtips, the Spitfire VI was optimised for high-altitude flying. BR579/ON-H of No 124 Sqn was used by Flt Lt Mike Kilburn to claim all of his victories with the Mk VI (via J D R Rawlings)

action again on 7 November when, over the Channel 30 miles south of Beachy Head, Sous Lt André Moynet bagged two Fw 190s in unusual circumstances;

'I could see my bullets striking the water behind the enemy aircraft. I closed to 300/200 yds, dead astern and gave a long burst. He turned sharply to the right and his No.2 collided with his tail. The No.1 went straight into the sea, but the No.2 tried to land on the water. However, he sank almost at once.'

Moynet later became an ace flying Yak fighters over the Eastern Front with the *Groupe Normandie*. The following day No 401 Sqn's Spitfire IXs escorted B-17s attacking Lille, and when two Fw 190s appeared Flt Lt Don Morrison led his wingman, Plt Off D R Manley, down to intercept them. More enemy fighters soon engaged the formation, and Morrison and Manley succeeded in shooting one down in flames before both pilots were overwhelmed by enemy fighters. Manley was killed and Morrison bailed out seriously wounded, German doctors eventually having to amputate one of his legs in order to save his life. At the time Don Morrison was the leading RCAF ace in Fighter Command.

Operations continued, although often at a reduced level as winter weather closed in. It was during a 'Rhubarb' over Belgium on 19 November that Flg Off André Plisnier of No 350 Sqn shot down a Bf 110 near Ghent to become the latest Belgian ace. However, that afternoon, on a 'Rhubarb' to Schouwen, Plt Off Peter Durnford's No 124 Sqn Spitfire VI was shot down by flak. It was his 137th operational sortie, and after 12 hours in his dinghy he drifted ashore to become a prisoner. Another ace was lost to flak on the 10th when 21-year-old Australian Plt Off 'Slim' Yarra of No 453 Sqn perished after his fighter was hit by fire from a flakship defending a convoy off Westkappelle, near Flushing, and crashed into the sea.

Two days later the Spitfire VIs of Nos 124 and 616 Sqns provided withdrawal cover to an Eighth Air Force B-17 raid on France. As the bombers headed back over the coast the second formation of Flying Fortresses was attacked. No 124 Sqn immediately engaged the enemy fighters, and in the resulting mêlée three Fw 190s were claimed. One fell to Plt Off Johnnie Hull and another to Flt Lt Mike Kilburn, who also shared in the destruction of the third Focke-Wulf. Both pilots thus became aces – the last to do so on the Channel Front in 1942.

That same day (12 November) the largely Dutch-manned No 167 Sqn claimed its first victory when future V1 ace Flt Lt Archie Hall shot down two Fw 190s, although another pilot was lost. The unit suffered a further loss the following afternoon when its CO of just four days, Battle of Britain ace Sqn Ldr Brian 'Sandy' Lane, was lost when his Spitfire VB (AR612/VL-U) was attacked by Oberleutnant Walter Leonhardt of 6./JG 1 and crashed into the sea 20 miles west of Schouwen. His death serves to highlight what a grim year it had been for the RAF over the Channel Front.

CHAPTER FOUR

THE ENDLESS OFFENSIVE

After a year of bitter fighting that saw neither side gain any real advantage on the Channel Front, 1943 was to see the Allies finally prevail in both North Africa and on the Eastern Front. In Western Europe, the burgeoning might of the USAAF's Eighth Air Force and its daylight bombing raids was to force the Luftwaffe to increasingly focus on home defence. Initially, however, little changed for Fighter Command's squadrons, with the non-stop offensive against the western boundaries of the Reich continuing in much the same vein as it had done since early 1941.

The first victory of 1943 over the Channel Front was claimed by Free Frenchman Lt Eugene Reilhac of No 340 Sqn, who shot down an Fw 190. Sadly, he was killed on 14 March 1943 in combat with JG 26 shortly after taking command of the unit (*J D Oughton*)

The Biggin Hill Wing was scrambled to intercept a major raid by *Jabo* Fw 190s and Bf 109s on 20 January, and the success it enjoyed during the operation was duly celebrated in the Mess afterwards. These pilots, who each claimed two fighters apiece, are, from left to right, Wg Cdr 'Dickie' Milne (Wing Leader), Sqn Ldr Hugh 'Sinker' Armstrong (Officer Commanding No 611 Sqn) and Adj Robert Gouby (No 340 Sqn). Only Milne would survive the war (*A P Fergusson*)

During the 20 January action Wg Cdr 'Dickie' Milne used his personal Spitfire IX BS240/RM to down an Fw 190 and a Bf 109 off the south coast (*A P Fergusson*)

The Spitfire IXs of Hornchurch-based No 122 Sqn (including BS461/MT-H) were also involved in the action on 20 January (*author's collection*)

The first Spitfire victory over the Channel Front in 1943 fell to No 340 Sqn when, during a 'Circus' to Abbeville on the afternoon of 9 January, Lt Eugene Reilhac shot down Fw 190A-4 Wk-Nr 2406 'Black 3' of 15./JG 26. Its pilot, Unteroffizier Ludwig Roth, was killed, as was No 340 Sqn's Sous Lt J Moreac. Reilhac claimed his second victory on the 13th, whilst No 611 Sqn's Flt Lt Franz Colloredo-Mansfeld, who was of Austrian ancestry, was credited with his first success when escorting a Ventura attack on Abbeville that same day.

Another émigré pilot and future ace to claim his first victory that month was Flg Off Hugh Godefroy of No 401 Sqn, who, though in the RCAF, had been born in Java and held Dutch citizenship. On the 20th, when on patrol off Beachy Head, he spotted a gaggle of Fw 190s over the Channel running for home after a 'tip-and-run' raid on the south coast. Climbing to their height, Godefroy engaged one of the fighter-bombers, which crashed into the sea. This raid had caused a major 'flap', as the No 611 Sqn diarist noted;

'All the Squadron pilots were at lunch when a Tannoy announcement reported that more than 30 enemy aircraft were approaching Biggin Hill from the southeast, being just seven miles away. As the pilots hurried to dispersal a number of Fw 190s crossed the northern end of the airfield almost at ground level. Within eight minutes of the announcement being made 12 Spitfires were in the air, led by Wg Cdr ["Dickie" Milne]. By this time the "bandits" were just north of Bromley, where they dropped their bombs, before making a dash for the Channel coast, still at very low level. Wg Cdr Milne took the Biggin Hill Spitfires IXs to a point over Beachy Head to try and catch the raiders on their way back to Abbeville.'

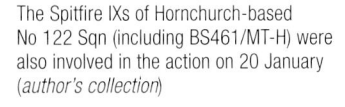

The ploy worked, and in the resulting 'bounce' 'Dickie' Milne, flying his personally marked Spitfire IX BS240/RM, succeeded in downing

an Fw 190 and a Bf 109F, whilst No 611 Sqn's CO, Sqn Ldr 'Sinker' Armstrong, got two Bf 109Fs that proved to be his final victories.

At 1245 hrs that same day Sous Lt Gouby of No 340 Sqn claimed two Fw 190s destroyed, thus making him the first ace of 1943. Just 15 minutes later No 91 Sqn CO Sqn Ldr Ray Harries also 'made ace' when he shot down a Bf 109 over Pevensey Bay. Shortly thereafter No 122 Sqn also engaged enemy fighter-bombers, with Sqn Ldr Don Kingaby claiming another fleeing Fw 190 – he had chased this aircraft across the Channel, shooting it down just as crossed the French coast. He was successful again the next day over Gravelines in poor weather;

'I went down on a F.W. 190 and opened fire at 400 yards astern, with cannon and machine gun fire, closing very fast, until I had to break away to avoid hitting the enemy aircraft. I saw hits all over its fuselage and then a sheet of flame, but had to break away to stop colliding with him.'

It was seen to crash by Flt Lt 'Wag' Haw, who also damaged another for his sole claim in a Spitfire.

At North Weald the two Norwegian squadrons continued to increase their reputation under the command of Wing Leader Wg Cdr 'Jamie' Jameson. As the Air Officer Commanding No 11 Group, Air Vice-Marshal H W L Saunders, commented, 'He put the seal of success on that Wing's career. Under Jameson they developed into first class fighters'. A number of pilots were regularly scoring victories, among them Lts Martin Gran and Svein Heglund and Capt Rolfe Berg of No 331 Sqn, all of whom made claims in early February.

The Canadians were also active at this time, and on 2 February *experte* Feldwebel Gerhard Vogt of 6./JG 26 was shot down by Spitfires over St Omer – he managed to bail out of Bf 109G-4 Wk-Nr 16129 'Brown 10' with severe wounds that hospitalised him for four months. His nemesis was almost certainly No 416 Sqn's Flt Lt Bob Buckham, Vogt being the future ace's second victory. On 15 February the docks at Boulogne and nearby Dunkirk were attacked by USAAF B-24s, which were in turn escorted by the North Weald Wing. The latter engaged Fw 190s that attempted to intercept the Liberators, Wg Cdr Jameson downing two German fighters for his final victories. Conversely, future No 331 Sqn ace 2Lt Leif Lundsten claimed his first success. His squadronmate 2Lt Helner Grundt-Spang also got a Fw 190, whilst No 332 Sqn's 2Lt Marius Eriksen shot down two – their claims made aces of both Norwegian pilots.

The following day one of the RAF's leading aces returned to action when Sqn Ldr Al Deere, flying with No 611 Sqn, participated in a 'Rodeo' to Hardelot, led by Wg Cdr 'Dickie' Milne. Fifteen Fw 190s were seen at 10,000 ft, and with No 340 Sqn remaining above to provide high cover, No 611 Sqn dived down, allowing Deere to gain his first victory in two years after following an enemy fighter into a dive;

'It was some time before I could get within firing range, and there was 480 mph IAS [indicated airspeed] on my clock when I opened with a short burst from dead astern at 200 yds. Pieces flew off the fuselage, and two further bursts

The highly successful Sqn Ldr Don Kingaby led No 122 Sqn into action on 20 January, claiming a Bf 109 destroyed. He followed this up with an Fw 190 destroyed and a second Focke-Wulf damaged the next day (*P Celis*)

On 15 February 2Lt Marius Eriksen of No 332 Sqn shot down two Fw 190s to reach acedom. He was one of the first two Norwegian aces, and when shot down and captured on 2 May he was his nation's leading scorer (*via Cato Guhnfeldt*)

produced many more pieces. He continued in his dive and went straight into the sea off Calais.'

There continued to be reverses, however, as the No 124 Sqn diarist noted for 17 February – 'A Black day, and one of the most unfortunate we have yet experienced'. The unit was covering a Ventura attack on Dunkirk harbour when, on turning for home, it was engaged by around 40 Fw 190s. Four Spitfires went down and three pilots were killed, including pre-war Kent and MCC cricketer Flt Lt Gerry Chalk and five-victory ace Plt Off Johnnie Hull. Ten days later, on a more positive note, three Fw 190s were shot down during another raid on Dunkirk. Plt Off Lorne Cameron of No 402 Sqn claimed one of these aircraft, having latched onto the tail of his victim and, after a number of strikes, watched it spin down and crash into the sea for the first of his six victories. No 403 Sqn's CO, Sqn Ldr Les Ford (also a future ace), got another.

SHAPING THE FUTURE

By the spring planning was in hand for the support of Allied armies after any landings in France. Tactical Air Forces (TAFs) were to be formed for this task, with the RAF supporting the Anglo-Canadian 21st Army Group. Many of the extant Spitfire squadrons would be transferred to fly in the fighter-bomber role, but to avoid disrupting continuing offensive operations units earmarked for this TAF would stay with Fighter Command for the time being. The reorganisation was to begin in the summer when Army Cooperation Command was absorbed, whilst Fighter Command would remain until the HQ of the Allied Expeditionary Air Forces was formed.

In early March Exercise *Spartan* was held to see if the experiences of the Desert Air Force in supporting the Eighth Army in North Africa could be applied to the battlefield in Western Europe. The exercise was also used to refine the overall TAF Command organisation. During *Spartan* some Spitfire units such as Nos 19 and 132 Sqns were mobile, operating from several austere sites, whilst others flew from permanent bases. One result of this exercise was the subsequent formation of mobile units known as Airfields (later re-named Wings) to which squadrons were allocated, and the establishment of an HQ for No 83 (Composite) Group within the 2nd TAF.

Whilst *Spartan* was on operations naturally continued. Indeed, Fighter Command participated in some notable actions during this period, such as on 8 March when Sqn Ldr Bill Crawford-Compton, now leading No 64 Sqn, shot down two Fw 190s for his first victories of the year, while his opposite number in No 122 Sqn, Sqn Ldr Don Kingaby got another. No 403 Sqn was also successful over France that same day, with future aces Flt Lt Hugh Godefroy and Flg Off Harry MacDonald each getting an Fw 190. The latter said of his first victory;

'I must have killed or wounded the pilot as his aircraft went into a gentle dive to the port, taking no evasive action at all. I turned to port, and from dead astern I kept firing till a large piece of the aircraft near the cockpit fell off. The port wing then crumbled up and broke away.'

The following day Sous Lt Pierre Laureys of No 340 Sqn shot down two Fw 190s, with a third destroyed on 14 March, to become an ace, whilst on the 11th Flt Lt Peter Howard-Williams, now with No 610 Sqn, also shot down a Focke-Wulf about three miles south of Beachy Head to claim his last victory. It also took him to acedom. The Norwegians also had a good day on 12 March when they made several claims, whilst a large operation on the 13th demonstrated the support the RAF was providing to the developing USAAF bomber offensive before the Eighth Air Force's own fighter escorts became fully established. The marshalling yards at Amiens were the target for 70 B-17s, escorted by 11 squadrons of Spitfires. While the Hornchurch Wing covered a feint towards Dieppe, claiming three victories, Spitfires from Northolt, Kenley and North Weald escorted the main attack and the Biggin Hill Wing provided target support.

The following day Wg Cdr 'Dickie' Milne was shot down and captured shortly after claiming his final victory. Three other pilots from the Biggin Hill Wing were also lost that day, including the new CO of Nos 340 Sqn (the promising Cdt Eugene Reilhac). Wg Cdr Al Deere became the new Wing Leader at Biggin Hill.

Early March also saw the service introduction of the new high-altitude optimised Spitfire HF VII with No 124 Sqn. Battle of Britain ace WO Garry Nowell flew one of the type's first operational sorties on 7 March when he scrambled in EN285/ON-Y after a suspected intruder. Further afield, off the coast of County Donegal, Eglinton's Station Commander, Wg Cdr Finlay Boyd, spotted a Ju 88 on 15 March that had flown up the west coast of Ireland reconnoitring the Atlantic convoy route. Off Malin Head Boyd got in a burst that set fire to the Junkers' port engine before it escaped into cloud – it was the 21-victory ace's final combat claim.

Three days later on the the other side of Britain, charismatic Coltishall Wing Leader Wg Cdr 'Cowboy' Blatchford and Nos 118 and 167 Sqns escorted Venturas of No 464 Sqn during their attack on the Maas sluice gates near Rotterdam. The bombers were attacked by Fw 190s from JG 1 off the coast near Voorne, at which point Blatchford used his superior height advantage to close on the No 2 aircraft in a pair of Focke-Wulfs. Hitting the fighter hard from 200 yards, he watched it enter an inverted spin prior to disappearing into cloud – Blatchford claimed a probable. Using his excess speed, he then closed on the leader and fired three bursts that struck the wing of the Fw 190, causing it to crumple and break off just as its pilot bailed out. The aeroplane was Blatchford's eighth, and last, confirmed victory. No 118 Sqn's pilots also saw some action, with Flt Lt Dickie Newbery (in EN966/NK-D) latching onto another Focke-Wulf and firing two bursts that shot its entire tail unit away for the first of his three victories.

During March the Kenley Wing came under the energetic leadership of Wg Cdr 'Johnnie' Johnson, who soon adopted Spitfire IX EN398. Decorated with his initials as his personal mount, Johnson would subsequently claim 17 victories (five of them shared) with this aeroplane

Flying Kiwis! In March 1943 the hugely experienced Wg Cdr Al Deere (right) became the Biggin Hill Wing Leader. With him is a rising New Zealand star, Sqn Ldr Johnny Checketts, who served under him in No 611 Sqn until being promoted to command No 485 Sqn (G A Jones via A P Fergusson)

Through much of 1943 the Canadian squadrons of the Kenley Wing were led by the dynamic Wg Cdr 'Johnnie' Johnson, who was to become the most successful Spitfire pilot of the war (via C H Thomas)

through the summer months. The first came on 3 April in the St Omer area during a 'Ramrod' when around 20 Fw 190s were spotted below the Wing in line abreast formation. Johnson led No 416 Sqn down to intercept them, the unit duly claiming three destroyed – one of these was the first victory for future ace Sqn Ldr Foss Boulton. Having engaged the enemy, Johnson then ordered No 403 Sqn, led by Sqn Ldr Les Ford, to attack a group of Fw 190s spotted to the right of the main formation. In the resulting general mêlée Ford became an ace;

'I closed in to 200 yards, giving a little more deflection, and fired again, seeing strikes on the cockpit. The enemy aircraft went over on its back, rolled slowly around as far as vertical and I fired again from close in. It went straight down in a flat slow spin and black smoke poured out.'

Among the other successful pilots was Flt Lt Charles Magwood, who took his first step to acedom. Les Ford shot down another Fw 190 near Rouen the next day and was then promoted to lead the Digby Wing, with whom he was killed attacking E-boats off Texel on 4 June 1943.

Fighter Command's units were now being increasingly employed as escorts for bombers participating in the growing daylight offensive against targets on the Continent, as the month of April clearly showed when Spitfires flew just over 3000 sorties in support of B-17s and B-24s, as well as No 2 Group's Bostons, Mitchells and Venturas. One such mission was undertaken on the 16th when No 616 Sqn's Spitfire VIs, led by future ace Sqn Ldr 'Pip' Lefevre, escorted USAAF B-24s for the very first time. Heavy flak was encountered and the CO's aircraft (BS114/YQ-C) was hit and crashed, although Lefevre survived and evaded to return to Britain three months later. No 616 Sqn endured some heavy losses during this period, as both of its flight commanders were killed during April (one fell to JG 2 on the same mission that saw Lefevre shot down).

For some of these raids Spitfires were fitted with unwieldy 30-gallon slipper tanks, as No 65 Sqn's Plt Off Peter Hearne (a future ace) described in the late 1980s;

'We were flying Spitfire Vs, each with a 30-gallon slipper under the belly. I had turned for home, flying low, when I noticed I was being chased by two Focke-Wulfs in line abreast. I opened the throttle to the gate but they still gained on me. Waiting until they were just outside effective firing range, I turned steeply to port, then came back onto my course for home. This simple manoeuvre, executed at the right moment, outwitted both aircraft. However, once again they were behind, catching me up, but this time they were in long line astern. I did not think the aircraft was travelling fast enough bearing in mind my throttle setting. I reached down for my slipper tank release toggle and pulled it again. The Spitfire seemed to leap forward, and I knew then the reason why those Fw 190s caught me so easily.'

No 118 Sqn's Sgt Clive Anderton had a similar problem when claiming his first victory on 4 April, as he recounted to the author;

'When we were attacked, despite pulling the toggle, I was unable to jettison the cumbersome external fuel tank with which our Spit Vs were fitted. I turned into four FW 190s and put the Spit into a climb and stall-turned. I managed a lengthy burst at one '190 as it passed beneath and saw the hood fly off and the pilot jump out.'

Johnson's aircraft at Kenley for much of 1943 was Spitfire IX EN398/JE-J, in which he claimed 17 victories (*via C H Thomas*)

The squadron had been covering a Ventura attack on Rotterdam that had met fierce opposition. One 'box' of bombers became separated and was coming under attack when Sqn Ldr 'Bertie' Wootten's section countered and he hit an Fw 190 in the engine, covering his Spitfire in oil. On the way home he had a narrow encounter with another German fighter that he also hit, these being the ace's final claims. That same day, leading No 167 Sqn, Wg Cdr Blatchford also damaged two Fw 190s. Claiming another Focke-Wulf as a probable on 2 May, Blatchford was killed on yet another bomber escort mission on 3 May. He had probably become the 18th victim of *experte* Oberfeldwebel Hans Ehlers of 6./JG 1, a future Knights Cross holder and 55-victory ace. He was replaced by ex-Malta ace Wg Cdr 'Sandy' Rabagliati, although he too was lost on 6 July 1943 whilst leading Typhoon-equipped No 56 Sqn (also part of the Coltishall Wing) in an attack on a convoy.

Six pilots, three Norwegians and three Canadians, became aces during May, the first being No 331 Sqn's Lt Helge Sognnes off Walcheren on the 2nd;

'A F.W. 190 dived down in front of me and as he pulled up I attacked. He saw me and started diving again so I followed. I fired several bursts. I saw cannon strikes on the fuselage and the aircraft started to smoke. I pulled out at 5000 ft when the enemy aircraft was diving vertically out of control. A few seconds afterwards, I saw a splash in the sea below me.'

The Norwegians were now flying Spitfire IXs, and in BS167/FN-L Lt Nils Jörstad claimed two Fw 190s for his first confirmed victories. However, Capt Marius Eriksen, who was the leading Norwegian pilot at that time, was forced down shortly after having destroyed a Focke-Wulf for his ninth victory. He spent the rest of the war as a PoW. A few days later No 402 Sqn, under Sqn Ldr Lloyd Chadburn, flew its first operation over the North Sea from Digby. Routinely flying with the Coltishall-based Spitfires, it regularly mounted 'Roadsteads' and anti-shipping 'Lagoons'.

It was a defensive scramble on the afternoon of the 9th that claimed the most significant 'scalp' of the period, however. A pair of No 165 Sqn Spitfires flown by American Flt Lt Art Roscoe and Sgt Scamen took off from Peterhead and intercepted Ju 88R nightfighter 'D5+EV' of IV./NJG 3. The aircraft, which had taken off from Aalborg, was flown by defector Oberleutnant Heinrich Schmitt. The Spitfire pilots escorted the aeroplane to Dyce, where, upon landing, the secrets of the nightfighter's radar systems were soon revealed.

Offensive work predominated during the spring months of 1943, however, and the Canadians in the Kenley Wing, led by 'Johnnie' Johnson, had a day of mixed fortunes whilst covering B-17s attacking Meulte on 13 May. By the time they approached the target around 50 enemy fighters had attacked the formation over Hazebrouck, allowing No 416 Sqn's Sqn Ldr Foss Boulton to destroy an Fw 190 for his fifth victory. Flg Off 'Jackie' Rae missed the call of 'Huns above', being left all by himself when the rest of the squadron broke formation;

'I found myself alone. I started to work my way out to the coast, and had reached a point about 15 miles in from Mardyck when three '190s attacked. I was able to turn inside the enemy without any difficulty and finally got into position to open fire on the last of the trio. Almost as soon as I tripped my guns, allowing one-and-a-half rings' deflection, the Focke-Wulf's wing tore away and he went down in a lazy falloff, streaming white smoke. His friends rolled away immediately. I got out.'

Rae was credited with his first 'confirmed', whilst Sqn Ldr Charles Magwood, now commanding No 403 Sqn, claimed his fourth. Also successful was a section led by Wg Cdr 'Johnnie' Johnson that was attacked over the Channel by four Fw 190s. A Bf 109 also joined in, and future ace Flg Off Harry Dowding (in BS540) of No 403 Sqn attacked it head on, hitting the cockpit and sending it crashing into the sea for his first victory. He also shared one of the FW 190s with Johnson and Flg Off Bowen. Later in the day, however, No 416 Sqn suffered a severe loss when, during another 'Circus' escorting a B-17 raid, Foss Boulton's Spitfire was hit, possibly by flak, at 26,000 ft over Amiens and he was forced to bail out badly wounded. Sqn Ldr 'Buck' McNair, a successful ace from Malta, replaced him. The next day (14 May), when No 416 Sqn's Flt Lt Bob Buckham flew to the aid of a crippled Flying Fortress, he shot the wing off an Fw 190 that then fell in flames to give him his fifth victory.

'1000-UP'

By mid-May RAF Biggin Hill's tally of victories since the start of the war stood at 998, and a sweepstake was run with a cash prize for whoever claimed the 1000th. On the 15th Wg Cdr Deere announced to his squadron commanders, 'An easy one today, chaps. Just a quickie over Caen'. He duly led the Wing, with Gp Capt 'Sailor' Malan as his No 3, on a freelance sweep in support of an attack on Caen airfield. No 611 Sqn was led aloft by Sqn Ldr Jack Charles while veteran pilot Cdr Rene Mouchotte was in command of Free French No 341 Sqn, which he had helped form five months earlier. In an incredible coincidence, both COs claimed victories – Charles two Fw 190s and Mouchotte one (his first) – and all three were shot down

Wg Cdr Al Deere's personal Spitfire IX EN568/AL sits in a blast pen at Biggin Hill in the spring of 1943. Flying it during June and July, he shot down an Fw 190, probably destroyed a second and damaged a third – these were his final claims (*G A Jones via A P Fergusson*)

so quickly it was impossible to decide who had put paid to the thousandth. Thus, at the debrief they split the stake!

That same day the high-altitude Spitfire VII was blooded when two aircraft from No 124 Sqn led by Flg Off Oliver Willis were scrambled from Exeter over the Channel. Willis later said of his significant victory;

'I was scrambled to intercept two bandits reported heading for Start Point at 1235 hrs. At 1310 hrs when approximately 60 miles southwest of Start Point, I opened fire on one of the two enemy aircraft from astern at 400 yards' range, seeing strikes on the fuselage and wing roots. The enemy aircraft was then lost to view, but I turned to re-engage and saw a parachute open and pieces of aircraft falling down to the sea.'

Although identified as an Fw 190, his victim was in fact a Bf 109G-4 of 4(F)./123 flown by Leutnant Wilhelm Marcks.

15 May also saw Flt Lt Harry MacDonald of No 403 Sqn attack a Bf 109 over France to decisively claim his fifth victory. 'I opened fire with a short burst, seeing strikes on the fuselage, including the cockpit and engine, and then the enemy aircraft fell to pieces, both wings crumpling at the wing roots'. He was joined a week later by Norwegian pilot 2Lt Olav Djönne of No 332 Sqn, who shot down an Fw 190 near Bruges from 17,000 ft. Sadly, one of his countrymen, Lt Rolf Tradin, was lost on 30 May whilst flying with No 611 Sqn. Over Pont Levecque during a 'Ramrod', a dogfight with Fw 190s developed resulting in the destruction of three Focke-Wulfs by Flt Lt Checketts, Sgt Lancaster and Lt Tradin. Minutes later, however, Tradin was shot down by another Fw 190. This aircraft was in turn destroyed by Sous Lt Pierre Laurent of No 341 Sqn. Rolf Tradin had claimed one of the few victories credited to Norwegian Gladiator pilots over Oslo in April 1940.

The first of Johnny Checketts' 14 victories was also No 611 Sqn's 100th;

'I attacked the FW190 from behind and below with an angle off of about 10 degrees to nil and saw heavy strikes on the fuselage and wings. The enemy aircraft appeared to stop and shed cowlings and pieces and smoke in dense clouds. I broke upwards and saw him spinning down smoking.'

Gradually, through the summer of 1943, squadrons were allocated to the newly formed Airfields as part of the strengthening of TAF. Nevertheless, from June until November cross-Channel operations remained under the control of No 11 Group. However, in anticipation of flying other operations following the invasion of France, these units were equipped and trained to be mobile, including practising living in tents. On 1 June at Coltishall, Battle of Britain ace Sqn Ldr Johnny Freeborn assumed command of No 118 Sqn, as he told the author;

'My part in 118 Squadron was for only a short time. Our work was mainly close escort to the American bombers of the Eighth Air Force. Other work was mainly with 2 Group day bombers – Bostons and Mitchells. My Flight Commanders were Tony Drew and Mike Giddings from units in Malta. Both were splendid men and excellent pilots.'

On 4 June Wg Cdr John Ratten, who had become the first RAAF Wing Leader in England when he took over the Hornchurch Wing from Irish Hurricane ace Wg Cdr 'Killy' Kilmartin just a few days earlier, shot

Spitfire VB EP120/AE-A provides the backdrop as Sqn Ldr Geoff Northcott (left), Officer Commanding No 402 Sqn, chats with Wg Cdr Lloyd Chadburn. Both men were aces, Northcott reaching this status whilst flying EP120 on 2 August 1943 when he shot down two Fw 190s (*Canadian Forces*)

down an Fw 190 during a 'Rodeo' to claim his fourth success. With the loss of Wg Cdr Les Ford that same day, Wg Cdr Lloyd Chadburn took over the Digby Wing. He would soon make it one of the best in Fighter Command. Future ace Flg Off Dan Noonan recalled, '"Chad" was a very special guy, a great leader, a friend to all and fun to be with'. Eventually, Sqn Ldr Geoff Northcott arrived to command No 402 Sqn, and he too would soon make his mark.

On 10 June No 167 Sqn flew its final operation as part of the Hornchurch Wing when it escorted a Mitchell raid on Ghent. During the course of the mission it tangled with Fw 190s of JG 1 and had two pilots killed. The unit then moved to Woodvale, where it became No 322 (Dutch) Sqn, although initially only eight of its pilots were from The Netherlands. It was commanded by Dutch-speaking SAAF pilot Maj Keith Kuhlmann, who had been credited with four victories over Malta.

After a three-year hiatus recovering from severe burns, Battle of France ace WO Garry Nowell returned to action when, at 0840 hrs on 13 June, he was scrambled in No 124 Sqn Spitfire VII MB813/ON-U and, off Ramsgate, shot down an Fw 190. The next day Nowell had the opportunity to talk with the German pilot he had brought down, asking him many technical questions regarding high-altitude flying.

Two days after this action, near Rouen, No 403 CO Sqn Ldr Hugh Godefroy shot down another Fw 190 to become the latest RCAF ace. However, on 17 June No 421 Sqn CO Sqn Ldr Phillip Archer (flying LZ996) was killed during a 'Rodeo' to Ypres shortly after he had downed a Focke-Wulf for his sixth victory. He was succeeded by the Malta ace Sqn Ldr 'Buck' McNair from No 416, who lost no time in opening his account with his new command when he spotted some Fw 190s near Doullens on 20 June;

'I fired a two-second burst at 350 yards, seeing strikes all over the cockpit and fuselage. His undercarriage came down and parts broke off and he started to burn and go down. I then gained height to reform the squadron.'

McNair was flying 'Johnnie' Johnson's JE-J on this occasion, finding the Mk IX the equal of the Fw 190. At Hawkinge, however, Battle of Britain ace Flt Lt Peter Parrott, newly arrived in No 501 Sqn, was less impressed with what he found;

'At the time we were flying cropped blower Spitfire Vs – "clipped, cropped and clapped" – which were very fast below 10,000 ft and hopeless above that height.'

Sadly, another ace was lost on 22 June when escorting Mitchells on a 'Ramrod' to Rotterdam, Lt Helge Sognnes of No 331 Sqn being shot down and killed. He was the only Norwegian ace to be killed in aerial combat. His compatriots soon redressed the balance, however.

Before the end of the month No 124 Sqn's high-flying Spitfire VIIs had seen more action when, early on 27 June, WO Garry Nowell (in MB820/ON-E) claimed his 11th and last at 30,000 ft east of the North Foreland. Having identified his target as an 'Fw 190', he used the superior speed of his fighter to close to within 150 yards before firing a two-second burst that sent the aircraft diving away in flames. His victim was actually a reconnaissance Bf 109 of 5(F)./123, flown by Feldwebel Heinz Sieker. Nowell was commissioned as a Pilot Officer two days later.

Further up the Channel that same day Lt Col Helge Mehre, who since May had led the North Weald Wing, was at its head near Flushing when he spotted Fw 190s far below. Mehre led the Norwegians down into an action that would make him an ace, later noting;

'I opened fire on one at approximately 300 yards, seeing cannon strikes all over the cockpit, engine and tail. Large pieces from the cockpit were soon falling off, and then the entire hood. A piece of the tail also broke off. The aircraft slowly went over on its back with smoke and flames and spun down.'

His and 'Johnnie' Johnson's Kenley Wing were among the most successful formations during this period, with a typical operation being a sweep on 1 July when No 403 Sqn destroyed a trio of Bf 109Gs. The successful pilots were Sqn Ldr Godefroy, Flg Off Norm Fowlow and Flt Sgt Graham Shouldice. Film from the latter's camera gun showed smoke billowing from the stricken Messerschmitt he had attacked as cannon fire exploded around the cockpit area. Leutnant Hans-Joachim Heinemeyer and Unteroffizier Albert Westhauser of 11./JG 26 were killed, but the third pilot survived.

Also on 1 July, as part of the preparations for the future, No 125 Airfield formed at Newchurch with Nos 19 and 132 Sqns. Like other Wings that formed during this period, personnel lived under canvas and practised operating under field conditions as they continued to fly missions over France. One of the major lessons from Exercise *Spartan* was the provision of adequate mobile communications to enable the timely passing of operational orders. Soon afterwards, on the 6th, the Kenley Wing was embroiled with 12 Bf 109s near Poix, resulting in No 403 Sqn's desert ace Flt Lt Wally Conrad claiming his first victory of this new tour. He fired at a fighter that turned violently and disappeared beneath him, having been hit in the wing roots and cockpit. The Bf 109 was seen to wallow and crash in flames. No 421 Sqn's Sqn Ldr 'Buck' McNair also claimed a Messerschmitt destroyed, and four days later he downed another Bf 109 for his fifth victory on the Channel Front.

Small-scale sorties continued to be flown too, such as when Flt Lt John Shepherd of No 118 Sqn led a 'Rhubarb' from Coltishall that destroyed a locomotive and damaged a barge. On 18 July the unit, in company with Nos 402 and 416 Sqns, provided an escort to Beaufighters that were undertaking an anti-shipping strike off the Dutch coast. No 118 Sqn hit the target convoy's fighter escort of five Bf 109s, and Flt Lt John Shepherd (in

When with No 403 Sqn at Kenley in the summer of 1943 Flt Lt Wally Conrad flew Spitfire IX LZ997/KH-A, in which he claimed three victories. However, after the last of these on 17 August he collided with his wingman and had to bail out of it when the fighter's tail came off. Conrad avoided capture and made his way back to England via Spain (*W A Conrad via C H Thomas*)

Although of indifferent quality, this photograph shows pilots of No 118 Sqn's 'B' Flight at Coltishall on 18 July 1943 in front of Spitfire VB EP549/NK-Q after an escort sortie over the Dutch coast. It had been flown on this mission by Flt Lt John Shepherd (rear row centre), who had shot down an Fw 190 and shared a second with Sgt Clive Anderton (rear right) to become an ace (*C Anderton*)

EP549/NK-Q) attacked one that blew up and shared in the destruction of a second – with Sgt Clive Anderton – that took him to acedom. Anderton, who had fired a long burst into the Bf 109G, had the satisfaction of seeing the Messerchmitt hit the sea and break up for his second victory. He received a DFM shortly afterwards. Also successful was Flt Lt 'Dickie' Newbery, whose final victory took his total to three and two probables. He would subsequently claim ten V1s destroyed the following year.

On 25 July No 118 Sqn combined with Nos 401 and 611 Sqns for a 'Ramrod' led by the new Coltishall Wing Leader, Wg Cdr 'Laddie' Lucas, that gave rear support to 12 Mitchells attacking Schipol. As the bombers left the target the Luftwaffe intervened and No 611 Sqn turned to engage. In the resulting action Plt Off Harry Walmsley claimed a Bf 109 destroyed for the first of his 12 victories. Sqn Ldr Jack Charles engaged an Fw 190, which exploded with such ferocity that debris damaged his Spitfire's engine, forcing him to ditch 25 miles off the coast. He was picked up by an ASR Walrus that evening and returned to Matlaske.

During a repeat mission to Schipol two days later Nos 118 and 611 Sqns were joined by Nos 402 and 416 Sqns from Digby, and they became involved with more than 20 Bf 109s. Several were claimed, including a first confirmed victory for No 402 Sqn's future ace Plt Off John Mitchner. No 118 Sqn's Plt Off 'Jimmy' Talalla, also a future ace, and Plt Off Roy Flight shot down one of the few Messerschmitts that got near the bombers. The share was Flight's fourth victory, but he was shot down and captured on 15 September 1943, thus failing to make ace.

No 485 Sqn was also over France on 27 July, providing high cover to USAAF B-26s. Led by Sqn Ldr Johnny Checketts, the unit became embroiled in a running battle over Rouen at 20,000 ft that lasted eight minutes and resulted in the squadron being credited with four Fw 190s destroyed without loss. Checketts, having quickly shot a fighter down in flames, then became separated from his section in the subsequent mêlée. As he flew over the French coast he sighted three more Focke-Wulfs below him, so he dived on them;

'They were at about 25,000 ft. I attacked the rear one from about 300 yards astern and saw strikes on the port wing. I then hit him just as he rolled over and he went down steeply with flames streaming from the fuselage and cockpit.'

These two successes took the 31-year-old New Zealander to acedom and started a purple patch for him, as by the end of August he had more than doubled his total – including three Bf 109s destroyed and a fourth as a probable over Lille on 9 August.

The squadrons of No 125 Airfield continued operations from their tactical sites during this period also. On a typical day's flying during the summer of 1943, Gp Capt Jamie Rankin led Nos 19, 132 and 602 Sqns as they escorted USAAF B-26s sent to attack St Omer airfield in the morning and Abbeville marshalling yards in the evening. They were opposed only by flak during both missions. In an indication of how fluid the new Airfield structure was, shortly thereafter No 19 Sqn re-equipped with Spitfire IXs and moved from Newchurch to Kingsnorth to join No 122 Airfield.

The Norwegians continued to claim regularly throughout mid-1943, with No 331 Sqn's Capt Svein Heglund becoming an ace on 29 July.

With 15.5 victories, all but three on Spitfires, Capt Svein Heglund of No 331 Sqn was the most successful Norwegian pilot of World War 2 (*S Heglund via Cato Guhnfeldt*)

He too enjoyed a run of success, and by the end of October had claimed eight more victories, most when at the controls of his favourite Spitfire IX, MA568/FN-L.

It was in mid-August that ex-Malta ace Flg Off Ray Hesselyn, flying with No 222 Sqn from Hornchurch, began his career over the Channel Front in some style. On the 17th, whilst over Belgium escorting USAAF B-17s on a raid on Germany, 12 Bf 109s from 3./JG 3 were seen below the heavy bombers. Diving after them, No 222 Sqn quickly shot down no fewer than five of the enemy machines. Two fell to 22-year-old New Zealander Hesselyn, who recalled;

'We had got below the eight [enemy fighters] and I climbed for the No 2, attacking from the starboard quarter. I saw strikes and the enemy aircraft poured smoke, rolled on its back and crashed eight miles east of Neuzen. I turned to starboard and saw another Me.109G. I closed in and fired from dead astern, damaging it. A further burst showed strikes on the fuselage and wings, the canopy and some pieces flew off and the pilot bailed out. Finally, I saw the tail break off and the enemy aircraft crash in the estuary.'

Amongst Hesselyn's squadronmates at this time was fellow Malta ace Flt Lt Pat Lardner-Burke, who, ten days later, also opened his account on the Channel Front when he shot down an Fw 190 over St Omer whilst flying his personal aircraft (MH434/ZD-B), which he had adorned with the name of his wife, Mylcraine. Having joined 240 B-17s near Berck at 26,000 ft, No 222 Sqn was called into action when nine enemy fighters attacked. Diving below the bombers to counter the German machines, Lardner-Burke fired on two Fw 190s in quick succession. He followed the second Focke-Wulf down until it crashed near Calais.

Another ace from the Mediterranean also resumed scoring in mid-August when Sqn Ldr 'Jas' Storrar, now in command of No 65 Sqn and flying his personally marked Mk IX MH358/YT-JAS, saw a Bf 109 over the Pas de Calais;

'The Hun did not at first realise I was behind him. I opened fire using full throttle and revs. He began to turn and, seeing me, dived down. I followed him down to 5000 ft, doing 480+ mph and firing. At 5000 ft the Me's lefthand aileron came off and it flicked over the vertical and went straight into the ground near Cassel.'

Losses of course continued, and during a 'Ramrod' on 27 August Cdt René Mouchotte, No 341 Sqn's successful CO, was shot down and killed by Fw 190s of JG 2. Five days earlier Lt Michel Boudier had shot down a Bf 109 near Douai to become the first pilot to reach acedom with No 341 Sqn. Another ace casualty came on 4 September when, during a 'Ramrod', Flt Lt Tony Gaze of No 66 Sqn became the 14th victim of Feldwebel Gerhard Vogt during an aerial engagement with Fw 190s of II./JG 26 over Ault. Although he suffered facial injuries during the crash landing, Gaze evaded successfully and made it back to England in late October.

No 403 Sqn lost its CO, Sqn Ldr Frank Grant, the same day. However, Nos 129 and 222 Sqns of the Hornchurch Wing enjoyed success on the 4th, as did Wg Cdr Lloyd Chadburn's Digby Wing. Among its scorers were future aces Flg Offs Art Sager and Dan Noonan of No 416 Sqn, who shared a Bf 109 to register their first victories. No 402 Sqn's Plt Off Leslie Moore and American Sgt Jim Thorne claimed an Fw 190 each as they

South African Flt Lt Pat Lardner-Burke joined No 222 Sqn as 'A' Flight Commander in March 1943, just prior to the unit being posted from Ayr to Martlesham Heath, and then on to Hornchurch. From late August of that year Lardner-Burke, who had 'made ace' in the defence of Malta in 1941, started routinely flying Spitfire IX MH434. He would duly claim 2.5 victories and one damaged in the fighter in the space of just 11 days (*via Chris Yeoman*)

On 4 September Capt Svein Heglund claimed a Bf 109 shot down and a second as a probable. The former was probably flown by *experte* Leutnant Kurt Goltzsch, *Staffelkapitän* of 5./JG 2, who made an emergency landing and suffered a serious spinal injury – he had to be lifted unconscious from the wreckage. Goltzsch succumbed to his injuries a year later (*Morten Jessen*)

too took their first steps towards acedom. Finally, Chadburn was also credited with his first solo victory, as No 416 Sqn's diarist described. 'He tore into the nearest Focke-Wulf head-on, giving it bursts from 400 yards to point blank, and saw the fighter crash on the cliffs north of Le Touquet'. In all 21 victories were claimed on 4 September.

During that morning, however, results had been more modest, with just a single Bf 109 being credited to Capt Svein Heglund, who also claimed as second as a probable. The latter was probably Bf 109G-6 Wk-Nr 20209 flown by 43-victory ace Leutnant Kurt Goltzsch, *Staffelkapitän* of 5./JG 2. He had to perform an emergency landing that resulted in him suffering serious spinal injuries. Lifted unconscious from the cockpit, Goltzsch eventually succumbed to his injuries a year later.

During his combat with Leutnant Goltzch, Svein Heglund flew Spitfire IX MA568/FN-L. He claimed no fewer than seven victories with the aeroplane between August and September 1943 (*S Heglund via Cato Guhnfeldt*)

The fighting of 4 September proved to be the precursor to several days of fierce aerial combat that resulted in many victory claims being made and nine Spitfire pilots becoming aces during the month. Among the latter was No 485 Sqn's WO Bert Wipiti, a Maori who had claimed four victories flying Buffaloes during the ill-fated defence of Malaya in January 1942 (see *Osprey Aircraft of the Aces 91 – Brewster F2A Buffalo Aces*). On 16 September, during a vigorous action whilst flying as high cover to Marauders attacking Beaumont-le-Roger airfield, the New Zealanders were attacked by a mix of Fw 190s and Bf 109s. These fighters tried twice to get to the bombers, but they were prevented by a section of six Spitfires from No 485 Sqn that dived on them and finally drove the enemy aeroplanes down almost to ground level. Plt Off Johnnie Houlton, himself a future ace, vividly described in his autobiography the desperate mêlée during which Wipiti became an ace;

'Bert spotted six '190s coming in from the right, and pulled round into them. I glimpsed a Spitfire wheeling around just above me (which turned out to be Bert) and could see the control surfaces on the '190 working rapidly as the aircraft was pulled round tight to judder each time it hit the point of high-speed stall so that our streaming vapour trails made a crazy pattern of irregular white arcs. I managed to pull through his flightpath to fire a short burst that produced a flurry of bright strikes on the wing root. As the '190 pilot flicked away into an opposite turn he flew right into Bert's line of fire, and a short burst smashed the aircraft down into the woods in a great shower of debris.'

Of his Maori colleague Houlton said, 'Bert was a bundle of energy, intent on getting to grips with the enemy under any or every circumstance'. Sadly, in a dogfight over the Somme Estuary on 3 October, moments after he had shared in the destruction of his sixth victory, the Maori pilot was shot down into the sea and killed. Another New Zealand ace was lost that same day when No 222 Sqn's Flt Lt Ray Hesselyn, on a 'Ramrod' near Beauvais, became embroiled with some Bf 109s. Having shot one down to achieve his 19th victory, he was then wounded in the legs. With his Spitfire on fire, Hesselyn was forced to bail out and became a PoW. Once in captivity he became a persistent escaper, for which he would later receive an MBE.

3 October also saw Wg Cdr Lloyd Chadburn's Digby Wing tasked with escorting Marauders targeting the Dutch port city of Ijmuiden. German fighters eventually appeared once the bombers were on their way home, the Wing diving on Bf 109s from out of the sun. Spotting a Spitfire being chased, Chadburn opened fire from 300 yards and watched the Messerschmitt's wheels drop down, before a second burst caused an explosion in the wing and the fighter descended through cloud into the sea. Malta ace Flt Lt Wilbert Dodd also scored his first victory with No 402 Sqn during the same engagement. Five days later No 402 Sqn claimed an unusual victim when, during an ASR patrol off the Dutch coast, four fighters from the unit spotted a Dornier Do 24 flying boat. Each taking turns to attack the aeroplane, it was finally despatched by Plt Off Leslie Moore in his second pass when he tore sections off the wing. The hapless flying boat crashed into the sea, thus providing Moore with the second of his six victories. Flt Lt Dodd's share proved to be his last aerial success.

Fighters in the west of England also saw regular action both on offensive and defensive sorties, such as on 13 October when Sqn Ldr Keith Lofts, CO of No 66 Sqn, led eight Spitfires on an 'Instep' patrol (a mission to counter attacks on Coastal Command aircraft over the Western Approaches). A Ju 88 was spotted about 70 miles southwest of Land's End and the fighters intercepted it before the bomber could reach cloud. Lofts and several others attacked the enemy machine, causing the Ju 88 to stall and then dive into the sea wreathed in flames. Lofts' share in its demise provided him with his sixth, and last, victory. It was also the sixth, and last, success for Malta ace Flg Off Arthur Varey.

At the end of October No 349 Sqn became the second Belgian-manned Spitfire unit to be declared operational, its CO, Sqn Ldr Yvan du Monceau de Bergendael, leading his charges on an escort mission for bombers targeting Beauvais airfield. This unit was earmarked for the planned 2nd TAF, as were Nos 19 and 122 Sqns, which, on the fine clear morning of 11 November flew a sweep to St Pol as a diversion for a raid by USAAF Marauders. They were jumped by more than 12 fighters, and Flt Lt T H Drinkwater of No 19 Sqn fired on an Fw 190;

'I turned and, using full boost and revs, chased him down from 17,000 ft and got in a couple of bursts from dead astern. I saw cannon strikes, but can't say where as my windscreen fogged up. I pulled up to about 3000 ft and, looking down, saw the '190 hit the ground and burst into flames.'

He had just achieved No 19 Sqn's 100th victory. Future No 122 Sqn ace Flg Off Alan Pavey was also credited with sharing in the destruction of an Fw 190 over St Pol during this mission, thus registering his first victory (achieving acedom in the Mustang III, he was killed in action on 27 July 1944).

These successes were virtually a swansong for Fighter Command's Spitfires as plans to reorganise the Allied Air Forces prior to the D-Day invasion came to fruition.

The last victories before Fighter Command was dissolved were claimed on 11 November 1943. Amongst those to enjoy success on this date was future ace Flt Lt Alan Pavey of No 122 Sqn, whose share in the destruction of an Fw 190 over St Pol was the first of his seven victories – the remaining six came in a Mustang III. He was killed in action near Caen on 27 July 1944 (via *C F Shores*)

CHAPTER FIVE

PREPARING FOR INVASION

On 13 November Air Chief Marshal Sir Trafford Leigh Mallory was appointed to command the HQ Allied Expeditionary Air Force (AEAF) that would comprise three elements. The USAAF's Ninth Air Force was similar in composition to the RAF's Tactical Air Force that formed the second element, whilst the remainder of Fighter Command was to be renamed as Air Defence of Great Britain (ADGB). On the 15th the TAF was formerly brought into being as the 2nd TAF, with its Nos 83 and 84 Groups having fighters under their command. In No 83 Group, No 122 Airfield (Gravesend), No 125 Airfield (Detling), No 126 Airfield (Biggin Hill) and No 127 Airfield (Kenley) controlled Spitfire squadrons, whilst No 84 Group had No 131 (Polish) Airfield at Northolt, No 132 (Norwegian) Airfield at North Weald, No 133 (Polish) at Heston, No 134 (Czech) Airfield at Ibsley and No 135 Airfield at Hornchurch.

All of the Airfields were led by highly experienced officers, many of whom were aces. The residue of the old Fighter Command squadrons continued with ADGB and its subordinate Groups (Nos 9, 10, 11 and 12) that remained as before. Initially, however, until HQ 2nd TAF became fully established, operations by units assigned to Nos 83 and 84 Groups continued to be controlled by HQ No 11 Group. Replacement of the Spitfire VB with the Mk IX continued apace, and within several weeks of each other in October-November Nos 401 and 412 Sqns had been re-equipped. In practice, at squadron level, little changed, with operations continuing unabated with

This Spitfire IX of No 411 Sqn, photographed at Biggin Hill in late 1943, was used by Flt Lt Doug Matheson to shoot down an Fw 190 near Ostend on 29 November. Two days later he was forced to bail out of another aircraft and became a PoW (via P H Listemann)

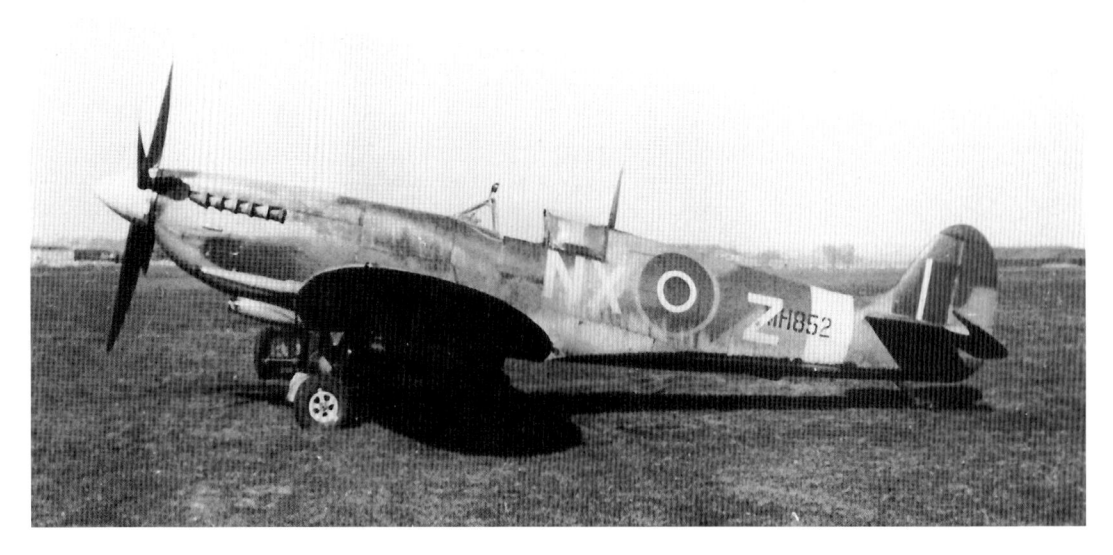

Part of the escort to USAAF B-26s on a 'Ramrod' on 1 December was provided by No 131 Sqn, whose Flt Lt Cliff Rudland flew Spitfire IX MH852/NX-Z on the mission. He was at its controls again four days later for a repeat mission (*K A Saunders*)

an increased focus on attacks on mysterious structures in northern France as the campaign against German secret weapons developed.

On 19 November over Normandy, 21-year-old Flt Lt Anthony Bradshaw of No 129 Sqn shot down an Fw 190 for his fifth victory, thus making him the first pilot to become an ace since the Command changes. Like so many before him, however, his was but a brief glory for during a 'Ramrod' on 22 December he collided with another Spitfire when avoiding flak over St Saens. Forced to bail out, Bradshaw spent the rest of the war as a PoW. He was the last ace lost over the Channel Front in 1943.

Despite the worsening weather, it was very much 'business as usual' during a Beaufighter attack on a convoy off the Dutch coast on 23 November when Flt Lt Johnny Plagis of the Coltishall Wing's No 64 Sqn shot down an Fw 190 off Den Helder for the Rhodesian ace's last victory of the year. No 416 Sqn was in action three days later when the Digby Wing, led by Wg Cdr Chadburn, flew a 'Ramrod' from Manston. Approaching Cambrai, four fighters were spotted taking off. Two Spitfires from No 416 Sqn were ordered down to intercept them, as Flt Lt Art Sager (in veteran Mk VB W3621) described in his autobiography;

'I saw four aircraft taking off from a small airfield below and behind. I reported them to Freddie [Sqn Ldr Fred Green] and he agreed my section could have a go, saying he'd cover us with the rest of the Squadron. We turned and dived, throttle through the gate, everyone close, catching glimpses of the Huns below the low scattered clouds. When we levelled out we saw they were FW 190s, three in formation flying toward a cloud and a straggler some distance behind. We got on the deck below him and caught up fast. Keeping the '190 squarely in the sights, I concentrated on the trim to keep from skidding, and when he was 50 yards away I fired with cannon and machine gun. It exploded, pieces going in every direction and the fuselage bouncing in flames over a railway embankment.'

The Fw 190 was flown by Leutnant Hans Fischer of 5./JG 26, Sager's fourth victory being No 416 Sqn's last for nearly six months.

That same day future ace Flt Lt Jack Sheppard of No 401 Sqn claimed his first success, as the unit diary described. 'Flt Lt Sheppard got the first

Hun since we've been on Spit IXs. Sheppard led his section down to the deck on a Jerry that had just taken off. After a five-minute chase, Sheppard destroyed the FW 190'. Sadly, four days later, No 401 Sqn lost both of its flight commanders when two aircraft were brought down with engine failure during a 'Ramrod' for B-17s. One pilot survived to become a PoW, but nine-victory ace Flt Lt Harry MacDonald perished. Having glided about halfway to the English coast after the Merlin in his Spitfire IX had cut out, he could not extricate himself from the cockpit of his fighter when he eventually tried to bail out about 30 miles from the Essex coast. The unit diary noted somberly, 'He was one of the Squadron's finest'.

BOMBER ESCORTS

By late 1943 Spitfire units from both the 2nd TAF and ADGB were providing cover for AEAF medium bombers on virtually a daily basis. Proving just how integrated operations had become, the escort for a 'Ramrod' by 54 B-26s of the Ninth Air Force on 1 December included the Spitfire IXs of ADGB-controlled No 131 Sqn flying alongside several 2nd TAF units. One of the sections was led by former Whirlwind I pilot Flt Lt Cliff Rudland, who had just returned to operations after a period as a test pilot.

When weather permitted, larger operations continued to be mounted, such as on 20 December when the Eighth Air Force attacked Bremen. In addition to escorts for the USAAF bombers, Spitfire units also flew many diversionary raids and sweeps. During the late morning Nos 403 and 421

Throughout the autumn of 1943 the Norwegian No 132 Airfield at North Weald was led by Dane Lt Col Kaj Birksted, who had become an ace in August. His first personally marked Spitfire IX was BS458/KB in which he claimed two victories during September (*Bengt Stangvik*)

Relaxing at North Weald after a sortie, Kaj Birksted (left) lights a cigarette for fellow ace Capt Leif Lundsten of No 331 Sqn (*via Tor Larsen*)

Sqns of No 127 Airfield encountered almost 40 fighters near Merville, and the CO of the latter unit, Sqn Ldr Jim Lambert, and Flt Lt Karl Linton each shot down a Bf 109. Linton's victory gave him ace status. A short while later Fw 190s from 4./JG 26 bounced the squadron, killing Lambert. He became the last squadron commander lost in 1943. Reacting to the loss of their CO, No 421 Sqn claimed four Focke-Wulfs shot down, including two to Flg Off Andy Mackenzie. He also destroyed a Bf 109 to achieve ace status in some style.

Further north, near Brussels, the No 126 Wing squadrons intercepted a formation of enemy bombers. No 411 Sqn downed a Do 217 whilst No 401 Sqn's Flt Lt Lorne Cameron continued on his path to acedom by destroying a Ju 88 near Lille.

That same day Lt Col Kaj Birksted led the Norwegians of No 132 Airfield on a sweep of the Cambrai area at 24,000 ft. A number of Fw 190s were engaged, Birksted (in his personal Spitfire IX MH830/KB) destroying one for his tenth victory and Lt Birgar Tidemand-Johansen of No 332 Sqn claiming another. A third fell to No 331 Sqn's Lt Fredrik Fearnley, who described achieving his fifth victory in his report. 'I closed in out of sun from port and above to 300 yards, giving two short bursts, and closing to 250 yards as I fired. I saw numerous hits around the cockpit and the enemy aircraft exploded – big pieces fell off, one of them hitting the leading edge of my port wing, causing slight damage'. Other Norwegian pilots watched the blazing remains crash into the ground.

Further attacks on 'Noball' (V1 flying bomb) sites were covered in the days before Christmas and, after a seasonal break, soon resumed in the final days of 1943. A No 350 Sqn aircraft was shot down by flak on a 'Rhubarb' on the 28th, killing its Belgian pilot, Flt Sgt G L M G Dancot – his was the last Spitfire to fall in 1943. Shortly after 1300 hrs on the 30th, near Albert, having returned from his incarceration in Italy, Malta ace Plt Off Claude Weaver of No 403 Sqn shot down a Bf 109. Flg Off Hartland Finlay got another for the first of his five combat claims. That same day No 412 Sqn was part of the escort for B-17s targeting the Compiègne region of France. During the course of the mission the greatest ace of the defence of Malta, Flt Lt George 'Screwball' Beurling, claimed an Fw 190 destroyed;

'I sighted a F.W. 190 cutting in from behind and below. I rolled to starboard and cut into the F.W. 190 which dived away. I took a long-range three-second burst. I closed and fired another one-second burst. The enemy aircraft rolled to starboard and I fired another burst. It went straight down in flames and I saw the pilot bail out.'

This was the Canadian's 32nd, and last, victory.

Action also continued in the west on 30 December shortly after eight Spitfires from No 341 Sqn took off in the early afternoon for an 'Instep' led by seven-victory ace Cne Pierre Montet. Northwest of Ushant they engaged four Fw 190s that turned to run for cloud cover, but not before three of them had been hit – two by Montet for his final claims.

The following day over St Brieuc, on the Brittany coast, Sqn Ldr 'Tim' Johnstone and his No 165 Sqn flew with the Culmhead Wing as rear target support for American heavy bombers returning from the Bordeaux area. When the squadron rendezvoused with the bombers some Fw 190s were seen, as Johnstone later recorded. 'I decided to investigate and dived down from 20,000 to 12,000 ft onto their tails and the aircraft was recognised as an F.W. 190. I opened fire at 150 yards with a one-second burst, breaking away at 50 yards. Cannon strikes on the fuselage were seen'. Others saw one of the Focke-Wulf's main undercarriage legs fall down as the fighter dropped away in an almost vertical spiral dive, smoking badly, before it burst into flames. Johnstone therefore claimed it as destroyed, and thus became the last Channel Front Spitfire pilot to 'make ace' in 1943.

Since January 1941 no fewer than 126 pilots had claimed five or more victories in the Spitfire over the Channel Front, whilst 259 more had claimed part of their total in the same period over an area that had seen some of the most protracted and intense aerial combat of World War 2.

One of the last victories scored by a Spitfire over the Channel Front in 1943 was also the 32nd, and last, credited to ranking Canadian ace Flg Off George 'Screwball' Beurling of No 412 Sqn (*via C H Thomas*)

Author's Note
Full details of the US-manned RAF 'Eagle' and USAAF Spitfire squadrons serving on the Channel Front can be found in *Osprey Aircraft of the Aces 80 – American Spitfire Aces*, whilst Polish units from this theatre are covered in *Osprey Aircraft of the Aces 127 – Polish Spitfire Aces*.

APPENDICES

SPITFIRE ACES OF THE CHANNEL FRONT 1941-43

NAME	SERVICE	UNITS	SPITFIRE CLAIMS 1941-43	TOTAL CLAIMS
Finucane B E F	RAF	65, 452, 602, Hornchurch Wg	24+6sh/6+1sh/7	26+6sh/8+1sh/8
Johnson J E	RAF	616, 610, Kenley Wg, 127 Wg	20+7sh/3+1sh/9+3sh	34+7sh/3+2sh/10
Rankin J	RAF	64, 92, Biggin Hill Wg, 15 Wg	17+5sh/3+2sh/16+3sh	17+5sh/3+2sh/16+3sh
Crawford-Compton W V	RAF	122, 485, 611, 64, Hornchurch Wg	16+1sh/3+1sh/12	21+1sh/3+1sh/13
Charles E F J	RAF	54, 64, 611, Middle Wallop Wg, Perranporth Wg	15+1sh/6+1sh/5	15+1sh/6+1sh/5
Malan A G	RAF	74, Biggin Hill Wg, Hornchurch Wg	13+3sh/1/9	27+7sh/3/16
Kingaby D E	RAF	92, 64, 111, 122, Hornchurch Wg, HQ Ftr Cd	13/4/5	21+2sh/6/1
Truscott K W	RAAF	452	13/3/3	14/3/3
Demozay J F	Fr	91	13/2/3	18/2/4
Heglund S	Nor	331	12+1sh/3/6+1sh	15+1sh/5/6+1sh
Duncan-Smith W G G	RAF	611, 603, 411, 64	11+2sh/5/2	17+2sh/6+2sh/8
Checketts J M	RNZAF	611, 485	12/3/7	14/3/8 & 2 V1
Broadhurst H	RAF	Hornchurch Wg	11/7/10	13/7/10
Armstrong H T	RAAF	129, 72, 611	10/3/2	10+1sh/3/2
Bader D R S	RAF	Tangmere Wg	8+3sh/5/5	20+4sh/6+1sh/11
Robinson M L	RAF	609, Biggin Hill Wg, Tangmere Wg	10/1/7+1sh	16/4+1sh/8+1sh
Rae J D	RNZAF	485	9+1sh/5/1	11+2sh/8+1sh/6
Birksted K	Dan	331, 132 Wg	9+1sh/-/5	10+1sh/-/5
Wells E P	RAF	41, 485, Kenley Wg	9/2/4+1sh	12/4/6+1sh
Eriksen M	Nor	332	9/2/3	9/2/3
McNair R W	RCAF	411, 403, 416, 421, 126 Wg	9/1/8	16/5/14
Chudek A	Pol	315, 303	9/1/1	9/1/1
Falkowski J P	Pol	315, 303	9/1/-	9/1/-
Maciejowski M M	Pol	317, 316	8+1sh/4/1	10+1sh/1/1
MacDonald H D	RCAF	54, 401, 403	7+2sh/1/5	7+2sh/1/5
du Monceau de Bergendael Count Y G A F	Belg	609, 350, 349	8/3/6	8/3/6
Gladych B M	Pol	303, 302	8/2/1sh	8/2/1sh
Jameson P G	RAF	266, Wittering Wg, West Malling Wg, North Weald Wg	8/1+1sh/2	9/1+1sh/2
Le Roux J J	RAF	91	8/1/4	18/2/8
Gouby R G	Fr	340, 165	8/1/3	9/1/3
Rigler T C	RAF	609, 610	8/1/2+1sh	8/1/2+1sh
Payne W J	RAF	610, 92	8/-/3	8/-/3
McColpin C W	RAF (US)	71, 133	8/-/2	11/-/3
Gaze F A O	RAF	610, 616, 64, 453, 129, 66, 41	7+1sh/4/5	11+3sh/4/5
Chadburn L V	RCAF	19, 416, 402, Digby Wg, Merston Wg	5+3sh/5+1sh/7+2sh	5+3sh/5+1sh/7+2sh
Stapleton F S	RAF	54, 611, Hornchurch Wg	7/4+1sh/4	7/4+1sh/3
Ruchwaldy D F	RAF	603, 129	7/3/6	7/3/6
Drobinski B H	Pol	303	7/1+1sh/-	7/1+1sh/-
Milne R M	RAF	92, Biggin Hill Wg	7/1/2	14+1sh /1/11
Grant R J C	RNZAF	145, 485, 65	7/1/-	7+1sh/1/-
Boudier M	Fr	340, 341	7/-/7	8/-/7
Northcott G W	RCAF	401, 402	7/-/3	8+1sh/1/7+1sh

Godefroy H C	RCAF	401, 403, 127 Wg	7/-/3	7/-/3
Montet P	Fr	341	7/-/2	7/-/2
Smik O	Czech	131, 122, 222	6+1sh/2/3	8+2sh/2/3
Hesselyn R B	RNZAF	234, 501, 277, 222	6+1sh/1/1	18+1sh/2/8
Buckham R A	RCAF	416, 421, 403	6+1sh/-/3	6+1sh/-/3
Thorold-Smith R E	RAAF	452	6+1sh/-/1	6+1sh/-/1
Grundt-Spang H G E	Nor	331	6+1sh/2/1+1sh	10+1sh/2/2+1sh
Chisholm K B	RAAF	452	5+2sh/-/1	5+2sh/-/1
Morrison D R	RCAF	122, 401	4+3sh/4+1sh/5	4+3sh/4+1sh/5
Peterson C G	RAF (US)	71	6/2/6	8/3/6
Skalski S	Pol	306, 316, 317	6/1/1	22/1/5
Pisarek M	Pol	315, 308, 1 Polish Wg	6/1/-	11+1sh/1/1
McKay D A S	RAF	91, 234	6/-/3	15/1/5
Ford L S	RCAF	412, 403	6/-/2	6/-/2+1sh
Archer P L I	RCAF	92, 416, 421	6/-/1	6/-/1
Janus S	Pol	308, 315, 1 Polish Wg	6/-/1	6/-/1
Adameck M	Pol	303, 317	6/-/-	6+2sh/1/-
Björnstad B	Nor	129, 331, 332	5+1sh/3+2sh/2+1sh	5+1sh/3+3sh/2+2sh
Lee-Knight R A	RAF	91, 610, 403	5+1sh/3/3	5+1sh/3/3
Brzeski S	Pol	317, 302	5+1sh/3/1	5+1sh/2/1
Sognnes H	Nor	331	5+1sh/1/10	5+1sh/1/10
Ortmans V M M	Belg	609	5+1sh/1/4+1sh	5+2sh/1/5+2sh
Christie W	Nor	332	5+1sh/1/3+1sh	9+1sh/1/4+1sh
Kilburn M P	RAF	124	5+1sh/-/4	6+1sh/-/4
Austeen A	Nor	124, 332, 64, 611, 331	5+1sh/-/3	5+1sh/-/3
Blake M V	RAF	234, Portreath Wg	5+1sh/1/-	10+3sh/-/+1sh
Gimbel E L	RCAF	401, 403, 421	4+2sh/1+1sh/1	4+2sh/1+1sh/1
Duperier B	Fr	340, 341	4+2sh/1/2+1sh	5+2sh/1/3+1sh
Koc T	Pol	317, 308, 303	3+3sh/3/-	3+3sh/3/-
Harries R H	RAF	131, 91	3+3sh/1/4+1sh	13+3sh/2/5+1sh
Dowding H J	RCAF	403	3+3sh/-/2	5+3sh/-/3
Bocock E P W	RAF	72, 602, 234	5/2/8	5/2/8
Boyd R F	RAF	54, Kenley Wg, Tangmere Wg, Eglinton	5/2/5	14+7sh/3/7
Gilmour W M	RAF	611, 54, 111	5/2/2	9/3/3
Mahon J B	RAF (US)	121	5/2/2	5/2/2
Bouguen M	Fr	340, 341	5/2/1	5/2/1
Spurdle R L	RAF	74, 91	5/1+1sh/5+1sh	10/2+1sh/9+2sh
Boulton F H	RCAF	416, 402	5/1/4	5/1/4
Hull B J	RAF	124	5/1/1	5/1/1
Rutowski K	Pol	306, 317	5/1/-	5½/2/1
Surma F	Pol	308	5/1/-	5/3+1sh/1
Mehre H O	Nor	331, 132 Wg	5/-/8	6/-/10
Magwood C M	RCAF	403, 421	5/-/3+1sh	5/-/3+1sh
Bowman H C F	RAF	129	5/-/2	5/-/2
Edner S R	RAF (US)	121	5/-/2	5/1sh/2
Poplawski J	Pol	308, 315	5/-/2	5/-/2
Durnford P E G	RAF	111, 124	5/-/2	5/-/2
Kent J A	RAF	92, Northolt Wg, Kenley Wg	5/-/-	12/3/2
Djönne O	Nor	332	5/-/-	5/-/-
Mitchner J D	RCAF	402	4/1+2sh/3	10½/1+2sh/3
Fearnley F A S	Nor	331	4+1sh/1+2sh/1	5+2sh/1+2sh/1
Gran M Y	Nor	331	4+1sh/2/4+1sh	8+2sh/2/5+1sh
Bradshaw A	RAF	120	4+1sh/1/2	4+1sh/1/2

Howard-Williams P J	RAF	118, 610	4+1sh/1/2	4+1sh/1/2
Linton K R	RCAF	416, 421	4+1sh/1/2	4+1sh/1/2
Lundsten L	Nor	331	4+1sh/1/1	4+1sh/1/1
Bache K	Nor	331	4+1sh/-/1+1sh	4+1sh/-/1+1sh
Zumbach J E L	Pol	303	4+1sh/3/1	12+2sh/5/1
Laureys P F	Fr	340	4+1sh/-/2	4+1sh/-/2
Mackenzie A R	RCAF	421	4+1sh/-/-	8+1sh/-/1
Fowlow N R	RCAF	131, 611, 403, 421	4+1sh/-/-	4+1sh/-/-
Scott-Malden F D S	RAF	603, 54, North Weald Wg	3+2sh/4/10+1sh	3+2sh/5/12+1sh
Mortimer-Rose E B	RAF	234	3+2sh/1/4+2sh	9+4sh/3+2sh/5+6sh
Saunders C H	RAF	92, 74	3+2sh/1/2	5+2sh/3/3
Dundas H S L	RAF	616	3+2sh/-/3	4+6sh/2sh/2+1sh
Woodhouse H deC A	RAF	610, Tangmere Wg	3+2sh/-/3	3+2sh/-/4
Marland R G	RAF	222, 603	3+2sh/-/2+1sh	5+2sh/4/3+1sh
Venesoen F A	Belg	350, 610	3+2sh/-/-	3+2sh/-/-
Mortimer-Rose E B	RAF	234	3+2sh/1/4+2sh	9+4sh/3+2sh/5+6sh
Colloredo-Mansfeld F F *	RAF	72, 611, 132	3/4/4	3/4/4
Niven J B*	RAF	602, 322	3/3/4	3/3/5
Shepherd J B	RAF	234, 118	2+3sh/1+1sh/2+1sh	8+5sh/1+1sh/2+1sh
Plisnier A M	Belg	350	2+3sh/1/3	3+3sh/1/3
Sewell H S*	RAF	54	4/2/-	4/2/-
Rettinger W*	Pol	308, 303	4/-/2	4/-/2
Prihoda J*	Czech	111, 313	3/1/1	4/3/2
Coen O H	RAF (US)	71	2+3sh/1+1sh/2	2+4sh/1+1sh/4
Ratten J R*	RAAF	72, 453, Hornchurch Wg	2+2sh/2+1sh/2	2+2sh/2+1sh/2
Rae J A*	RCAF	416	2+2sh/-/3	2+2sh/-/3
Daley W J*	RAF (US)	121	2+1sh/-/3	2+1sh/-/3
Killian R J C *	RNZAF	485, 222, 122, 504	2+1sh/-/3	2+1sh/-/3
Duke-Woolley R M B	RAF	124, Debden Wg, 4th FG USAAF	2+1sh/1/-	4+3sh/1/2+1sh
Donahue A G*	RAF (US)	64, 91	2/2/1	2/2/1
Boussa A L*	Belg	130, 124, 350	2/1/1	2/1/1

* Pilots that appear in the Grub Street volumes *Aces High*, *Those Other Eagles* or *Stars & Bars* and who have less than five victories, but where there is uncertainty as to their actual total

COLOUR PLATES

1
Spitfire IB X4272/QJ-D of Flg Off A C Bartley, No 92 Sqn, Manston, 3 February 1941

X4272 was one of the rare Spitfire IBs fitted with drum-fed 20 mm cannon that were delivered to No 92 Sqn in late 1940. Whilst at its controls on a patrol over the Thames Estuary on 3 February 1941, Flg Off Tony Bartley shot down He 111 'A1+AN' of 6./KG 55 off Southend for his ninth victory. This was his last success with No 92 Sqn and the unit's first in 1941. X4272 was later modified at Rolls-Royce into an interim Spitfire VB, and the fighter ended its days on test work at Supermarine.

2
Spitfire IIA P7916/SO-B of Sgt W J Johnson, No 145 Sqn, Tangmere and Merston, February-June 1941

Sgt W J 'Bill' Johnson, who joined No 145 Sqn at the end of the Battle of Britain, regularly flew P7916/SO-B throughout the spring and early summer of 1941. The fighter was delivered to the unit on 22 February and it left No 145 Sqn on 1 June. Remarkably, it survived until January 1945. On 1 March Flt Lt Mike Newling was flying P7916 when he shared in the destruction of a Ju 88 over the Channel. P7916 was crash landed by Johnson on 27 March, although he flew it again just three days later following hasty repairs. The fighter was a presentation aircraft named *Hinkley*, above which it wore the de Montfort coat of arms surrounded anti-clockwise with the letters HMAH (Hosiery Manufacturers Association of Hinckley).

3
Spitfire IIA P7666/KL-Z of Plt Off J Stokoe, No 54 Sqn, Southend, 20 April 1941

A presentation aircraft named *Observer Corps*, P7666 was initially delivered to No 41 Sqn on 21 November 1940 and used by the CO,

Sqn Ldr Don Finlay, to claim victories on 23 and 27 November – the latter success making him an ace. P7666 was transferred to No 54 Sqn on 22 February 1941, where it was coded KL-Z. During one sortie it was attacked by Bf 109s, and when its pilot dived to zero feet one of the pursuing fighters flew straight into the sea. On 20 April Plt Off Jack Stokoe was scrambled in it over the Thames Estuary, and he duly shot down a Bf 110 to claim his seventh victory. However, he was then attacked by escorting Bf 109s of JG 51 and forced to bail out off Harwich.

4
Spitfire IIA P7753/QJ-X of Flg Off L H Casson, No 616 'South Yorkshire' Sqn, Tangmere, 5 May 1941

P7753 was initially delivered to No 65 Sqn before transferring to No 616 Sqn on 26 February 1941, where it was coded QJ-X and, being a presentation aircraft, named *Pampero I*. 'Buck' Casson had joined No 616 Sqn pre-war and served with the unit throughout the Battle of Britain, during which he scored consistently. On 5 May 1941 Casson was scrambled in P7753 in company with Plt Off Roy Marples, and over the Channel off Littlehampton they attacked and damaged a Ju 88. However, return fire struck Casson's aircraft, causing a glycol leak, and he was forced to bail out over the coast. Casson immediately returned to operations and became an ace in July, only to be shot down over France the following month and made a PoW.

5
Spitfire IIA P8376/NK-Z of Flg Off P I Howard-Williams, No 118 Sqn, Ibsley, May-June 1941

P8376 was a gift aircraft from the Netherlands East Indies, being named *Sinaboong*. It was delivered to No 118 Sqn on 13 May 1941 and allocated to Flg Off Peter Howard-Williams, who had joined the unit at the same time. He christened the fighter *Sheila*, the name being applied to the cockpit access door. The aircraft also carried a white panel with a labrador's head silhouette. Although Howard-Williams flew P8376 regularly, another pilot was at the controls when it collided over Hampshire with P8368 and crashed. Howard-Williams made his first claim soon afterwards, and became an ace in 1943.

6
Spitfire VB P8749/DW-G of Flg Off F A O Gaze, No 610 'County of Chester' Sqn, Westhampnet, 10 July 1941

Tony Gaze joined No 610 Sqn in March 1941 and made his first claims in June. P8749, which was one of a batch of Spitfire IIAs that were built as Mk VBs, was initially delivered to No 610 Sqn. Gaze flew DW-G on a sweep on 10 July, and near Hardelot he got onto the tail of a Bf 109F which evaded so violently that it crashed into the ground to become the Australian's fourth victory. Gaze made ace in 1942, whilst P8749, following a period with No 129 Sqn, returned to No 610 Sqn and was eventually lost when it crashed into the sea off Scarborough on 16 March 1942.

7
Spitfire VB W3380/RN-J of Sqn Ldr D F B Sheen, No 72 Sqn, Gravesend and Biggin Hill, July-October 1941

After serving with No 74 Sqn, W3380 was transferred to No 72 Sqn in early July. Here, having become RN-J, it was adopted by the CO, Sqn Ldr Des Sheen. Flying it on offensive operations, he made several claims – firstly, a Bf 109 damaged off the French coast on 17 August, followed by another on the 20th. On 27 September Sheen used W3380 to lead 'Circus 103B', and on 2 October he probably destroyed a Bf 109E with it over Abbeville for his last claim. W3380 was damaged in an accident whilst being flown by another pilot shortly thereafter, though like Sheen it survived the war.

8
Spitfire VB W3628/XT-P of Sgt D P Lamb, No 603 'City of Edinburgh' Sqn, Hornchurch, August-September 1941

Presented as a gift from the people of Oman, W3628 wore the name in both English and Arabic under the cockpit. It was regularly flown through the late summer on offensive operations over France by future ace Sgt Deryck Lamb. Indeed, he was at W3268's controls on 4 September when, over the sea near Dunkirk, he shot down a Bf 109E and damaged a second to register the first of his nine victories. Lamb survived the war but *Oman* was lost in a crash during a test flight in 1942 when serving with No 303 Sqn.

9
Spitfire VB W3579/OU-Q of Flt Lt S C Norris, No 485 Sqn RNZAF, Redhill and Kenley, August-October 1941

Pre-war pilot Stan Norris 'made ace' in 1940 flying with No 610 Sqn and became a flight commander in No 485 Sqn when it was formed. Appropriately for an RNZAF unit, W3579 was presented by New Zealand and was named *Southland II*, arriving on 7 August. It was flown regularly by Norris, who, on 29 August, shot down a Bf 109F with it near Dunkirk during a 'Circus' to claim his eighth victory. On 31 October, while being flown by Kenley Wing Leader Wg Cdr Norman Ryder on a 'Circus', W3579 was hit by flak and its pilot forced to land on a beach near Dunkirk. Ryder duly became a PoW.

10
Spitfire IIB P8505/UO-H of Sgt E S Dicks-Sherwood, No 266 Sqn, Wittering, 18 September 1941

Presented by the people of Stamford and also wearing the town's coat of arms (on the left side of its fuselage), P8505 originally served with No 222 Sqn prior to being transferred to No 266 Sqn on 4 September. It also carried the name *Eva III* below the cockpit. No 266 Sqn was largely manned by Rhodesian pilots, one of whom was future ace Sgt Eric Dicks-Sherwood, who, on 18 September, was flying P8505 as No 2 to Wg Cdr Jameson (the Wittering Wing Leader) for an attack on the Dutch port of de Kooy. Approaching the coast, they were bounced by four Bf 110s, one of which the 24-year-old Rhodesian managed to damage for his first claim. However, both Spitfires received damage themselves. P8505 later served with Nos 65, 616 and 54 Sqns, before being used for training. It was eventually written off in a crash in June 1943.

11
Spitfire VB W3507/DV-S of Plt Off J H Whalen, No 129 Sqn, Tangmere, September 1941

Canadian Plt Off Jimmy Whalen joined No 129 Sqn in the summer of 1941, and this aircraft soon became his regular mount. He decorated it with a gold wreath around a fist, below which was a scroll featuring the rousing mantra *Victory is ours*. Whalen was flying W3507 on 17 September when, in a fight over the sea off Le Touquet, he shot down two Bf 109s. He was at the controls of a different aircraft (DV-R) four days later when, over the Channel, he shot down another Messerschmitt and damaged a second – his victory from this mission was reflected on W3507's scoreboard beneath the cockpit. Jimmy Whalen became an ace over Ceylon on 5 April 1942 whilst flying a Hurricane IIB with No 30 Sqn. He was eventually shot down by flak and killed in Burma on 18 April 1944 while flying a No 34 Sqn Hurricane IIB. Unlike its pilot, W3507 survived the war and was scrapped in 1948.

12
Spitfire VB W3821/UD-D of Plt Off R E Thorold-Smith, No 452 Sqn RAAF, Kenley and Redhill, September-November 1941

Former medical student Raymond 'Throttle' Thorold-Smith from Sydney joined the first RAAF Spitfire squadron upon its formation. He claimed his first victory in early August and from then on regularly added to his tally. By the time W3821 was delivered on 11 September his score had risen to two and one shared destroyed. Thorold-Smith was at its controls on 13 October when, inland of the French coast near Hardelot, he shot down a Bf 109F to reach acedom. He was also flying it on 6 November when, off Cap Gris Nez, he claimed a Bf 109 and an Fw 190 for his final victories. Thorold-Smith became the CO of No 452 Sqn in early 1942 and took the unit back to Australia, where he was killed in action attempting to intercept Japanese aircraft raiding Darwin on 15 March 1943.

13
Spitfire VB P8783/YO-A of Sgt D R Morrison, No 401 Sqn RCAF, Biggin Hill, November 1941-February 1942

Sgt Don Morrison from Toronto joined No 401 Sqn in the autumn of 1941 and soon began flying P8783 from Biggin Hill on a regular basis. It was decorated on the nose with the popular cartoon character 'Jiggs', and thus adorned, he made his first seven claims in the fighter starting on 18 November, when he shared in a probable Bf 109F. Morrison achieved his first victory four days later when he shot down an Fw 190 and damaged a second Focke-Wulf. He shot down a Bf 109F and damaged a second Messrschmitt fighter on 8 December. Continuing to fly this aircraft into 1942, Morrison shared in the destruction of a Bf 109 during the 'Channel Dash' on 12 February and claimed a probable Fw 190 two weeks later. These were his final successes in the aircraft. Morrison continued scoring throughout much of 1942, with his share in an Fw 190 on 8 November taking his tally to 11. However, he was badly wounded during this action and forced to bail out into captivity.

14
Spitfire VB W3848/JU-H of Sgt P E G Durnford, No 111 Sqn, Debden, December 1941-February 1942

When, in the autumn of 1941, No 111 Sqn was switched to nightfighting duties, its Spitfire VBs were painted overall black and given other modifications for the role – the colours were retained until March 1942. Sgt Peter Durnford regularly flew W3848 throughout this period, and during the 'Channel Dash' on 12 February he probably destroyed a Bf 109 over the German fleet to register his first claim. W3848 was also flown by future aces Sgt Tony Jonssen (who was the RAF's only Icelandic pilot) and Plt Off Gray Stenborg. Both W3848 and Peter Durnford survived the war.

15
Spitfire VB BL444/ZP-D of Plt Off A E Umbers, No 74 Sqn, Long Kesh, Northern Ireland, January-March 1942

New Zealander 'Spike' Umbers joined No 74 Sqn in August 1941 and remained with the unit until 1942, later becoming an ace when flying the Typhoon and Tempest. BL444 joined No 74 Sqn just after it had moved to Northern Ireland in late January 1942, and Umbers first flew it on the 29th when he conducted a cannon test. He then flew it no fewer than 19 times during February, including a scramble after an unidentified aircraft on the 15th. He performed his last sortie in BL444 11 days later. No 74 Sqn's CO, Battle of Britain Hurricane ace Sqn Ldr Pete Matthews, and future ace Plt Off Alistair Wilson also flew BL444 during its brief time with No 74 Sqn, as on 20 March it was written off in a crash.

16
Spitfire VB AD298/GQ-G of Sqn Ldr K T Lofts, No 134 Sqn, Eglinton, February 1942

When No 134 Sqn returned from the RAF's expedition to the Soviet Union in late 1941, it was re-equipped with Spitfires, one of which was AD298 that was adopted by the CO (note the fighter's rank pennant), Sqn Ldr Tony Millar. When he handed over command in February 1942, he passed it on to his successor, Battle of Britain ace Sqn Ldr Keith Lofts. During January and February it was also flown occasionally by Flg Off Neil Cameron, who already had several victories to his name and subsequently 'made ace' over Burma in 1945. Post-war, he rose through the ranks to become the Chief of the Air Staff. AD298 was passed on to No 81 Sqn in early April and was subsequently lost in a mid-air collision on operations serving with No 453 Sqn RAAF on 11 October.

17
Spitfire VB BL351/BP-H of Flt Lt J A A Gibson, No 457 Sqn RAAF, Andreas, Isle of Man, February 1942

On entering service, BL351 was allocated to the Australian-manned No 457 Sqn on 11 December 1941, and it was used by the unit during work-ups on the Isle of Man. The fighter was initially flown by Plt Off Ken James, who would later achieve 2.5 victories. On 31 December it was flown by Flt Lt Harold North on one of No 457 Sqn's last sorties of the year. In February 1942 BL351 was allocated to Flt Lt Johnny Gibson, a New Zealander who had been credited with 11.5 victories in 1940 flying Hurricanes with No 501 Sqn. The aircraft carried his impressive tally and the 'Donald Duck' motif he adopted as his own personal marking forward of the cockpit. BL351 was transferred to No 452 Sqn in March 1942 and eventually lost in a collision on the ground on 8 May that same year.

18
Spitfire VB BL973/RY-S of Flt Lt S B Fejfar, No 313 (Czechoslovak) Sqn, Hornchurch and Fairlop, March-May 1942

Pre-war Czech pilot Stanislav Fejfar served throughout the Battles of France and Britain, during which he became an ace. He later joined No 313 Sqn and became a flight commander, and when BL973 was delivered new to the unit on 30 March he adopted it as his aircraft. The Spitfire was decorated with Fejfar's colourful dog motif and his scoreboard, but, interestingly, not a Czech Air Force roundel. He flew BL973 regularly and made several claims when at the controls of the fighter. Indeed, Fejfar was flying it over Lille on 5 May when he was in combat with Fw 190s of III./JG 26 and shot one down and probably destroyed another. However, he was then shot down and killed by *Gruppenkommandeur* Hauptmann Josef 'Pips' Priller, becoming the German's 70th victim.

19
Spitfire VB BM124/LO-W of Sqn Ldr B E A Finucane, No 602 'City of Glasgow' Sqn, Kenley and Redhill, March-June 1942

The most successful Spitfire pilot over the Channel Front was Irishman Sqn Ldr 'Paddy' Finucane who, in January 1942, was appointed as the CO of No 602 Sqn. After recovering from leg wounds inflicted in combat with an Fw 190 on 20 February, he adopted BM124 as his own after it was delivered on 16 March. The fighter was a presentation aircraft from the people of Tonga, being named after the island nation's long-reigning monarch Queen Solote. Finucane eschewed personal scores on aircraft, although in addition to No 602 Sqn's lion marking he adorned BM124 with a shamrock to show his Irish roots and a bottle of champagne just for good measure! He saw much action at its controls over France, claiming four victories, four probables and four damaged with the fighter between late March and early June. Unlike Finucane, who was killed on 15 July, BM124 survived the war.

20
Spitfire VB AB202/SM of Wg Cdr F D S Scott-Malden, North Weald Wing, North Weald, March-August 1942

In March 1942 Cambridge graduate David Scott-Malden became the North Weald Wing Leader, and through the spring and summer of that year he flew at the head of his Wing at the controls of AB202. As was the privilege of his post, the aircraft carried his initials in place of unit code letters. North of St Omer on 28 April Scott-Malden probably destroyed an Fw 190, and over the next two months he claimed another probable, three damaged and, on 19 June, an Fw 190 shared destroyed all in AB202. Ten days later, when over Hazebrouck, he shared in the destruction of another Focke-Wulf to take him to acedom. Scott Malden made his final claim in AB202 during the Dieppe raid when he damaged a Do 217 bomber.

21
Spitfire VB BM579/FN-B of Capt R A Berg, No 331 (Norwegian) Sqn, Manston and North Weald, July 1942

One of a number of successful Norwegian fighter leaders, Rolfe Arne Berg served in No 331 Sqn for much of 1942 and, from June, flew BM579. For Operation *Rutter*, the postponed July raid on Dieppe, special nose stripes were applied to participating aircraft, as shown here. However, they had been removed by the time the raid actually took place on 19 August. That day Berg flew BM579 over the beaches, and during a series of fiercely fought engagements with Fw 190s he claimed two damaged and one destroyed – the latter was his first victory. However, BM579 was also hit and Berg was forced to bail out. He was quickly rescued from the sea.

22
Spitfire VB EN794/MN-X of Flt Lt Count Y G A F du Monceau de Bergendael, No 350 (Belgian) Sqn, Redhill, Southend and Hornchurch, July-December 1942

One of a number of presentation aircraft from the Belgian Congo, EN794 was named *Usoke* after a World War 1 action in German East Africa and, appropriately, was issued to the Belgian-manned No 350 Sqn on 5 June 1942. It was adopted by flight commander Flt Lt Yvan du Monceau de Bergendael, who had become an ace just five days earlier. He flew it regularly throughout the rest of the year, making his first claims in EN794 in late July. When over Dieppe on 19 August, the Belgian shot down an Fw 190 to claim his sixth victory, and this is how the aircraft is depicted here – he claimed two more victories in it later in the year. Whilst its pilot survived the war, *Usoke* was lost in an accident on 24 June 1944.

23
Spitfire VI BR579/ON-H of Flt Lt M P Kilburn, No 124 Sqn, Gravesend, Debden and Martlesham Heath, August-December 1942

One of only 100 Spitfire VIs built for high-altitude operations, BR579 was delivered to No 124 Sqn on 19 July 1942. It first saw action in the hands of Flt Lt Mike Kilburn, who shot down an Fw 190 with the aeroplane during the Dieppe operation. BR579 subsequently became his regular aircraft, and he used it to claim another Focke-Wulf on 29 August. Through the autumn Kilburn often flew the aircraft on escort missions, and during one such flight on 12 December, covering USAAF B-17s, he shared in the destruction of an Fw 190 to take him to acedom. Minutes later Kilburn engaged another Focke-Wulf and shot it down too. This made him the most successful Spitfire VI pilot and BR579 the most successful individual aircraft.

24
Spitfire IX BS548/GW-B of Sous Lt A Moynet, No 340 (French) Sqn, Biggin Hill, 1 December 1942

Originally built as a Mk V, BS548 was converted into a Mk IX before delivery and sent to the Free French-manned No 340 Sqn that was part of the crack Biggin Hill Wing on 7 November 1942. It thus wore the Cross of Lorraine marking beneath the cockpit. On 1 December the fighter was being flown by Sous Lt André Moynet over the Pas de Calais area when he became embroiled with Fw 190s of JG 26. Following the ensuing combat he was credited with destroying one Focke-Wulf and damaging a second. This proved to be Moynet's last victory over Western Europe, although he later became an ace flying Yaks on the Eastern Front. BS548 subsequently served with No 341 (French) Sqn until it was shot down by German fighters near Le Havre on 17 April 1943.

25
Spitfire IX BR369/EH-T of Wg Cdr E H Thomas, Biggin Hill Wing, Biggin Hill, December 1942

Another aircraft that was built as a Mk V but converted into a Mk IX, BR369 was notionally on the strength of No 340 Sqn at Biggin Hill following its delivery to the Kent airfield on 29 November 1942. However, it was allocated to Wing Leader Wg Cdr Eric Thomas, who had become an ace the previous month, as his personal mount. The aircraft is depicted here in the standard scheme as displayed during a press day with No 611 Sqn on 18 December. Eric Thomas was posted soon afterwards, and after modifications BR369 served with No 341 Sqn until it was wrecked in a landing accident on 25 March 1943.

26
Spitfire IX BS240/RM of Wg Cdr R M Milne, Biggin Hill Wing, Biggin Hill, January-March 1943

Pre-war pilot 'Dickie' Milne became an ace during the Battle of Britain, and in January 1943 he started his fourth frontline tour as the Wing Leader at Biggin Hill. He was allocated BS240 as his personal mount, and it carried his rank pennant, initials and the Cross of Lorraine. The latter was present beneath the cockpit as the fighter notionally 'belonged' to No 340 Sqn. On 20 January Milne was flying it when he shot down an Fw 190 and a Bf 109 off the Kent coast after a large-scale *jabo* raid. He regularly led his Wing in BS240, and on 14 March over France he used it shoot down an Fw 190 for his 15th victory. However, Milne's aircraft was also hit, and he bailed out into the Channel and was picked up by a German patrol vessel.

27
Spitfire IX BS451/FY-V of Flt Lt F F Colloredo-Mansfeld, No 611 'West Lancashire' Sqn, Biggin Hill, 14 March 1943

Of Austrian parentage, Franz Colloredo-Mansfeld became a flight commander in No 611 Sqn at Biggin Hill in late 1942 following a tour with No 72 Sqn. Through the first half of 1943 on operations over the Channel Front he saw action regularly, making a significant number of claims. However, Colloredo-Mansfeld's sole success in BS451 came over the French coast near Boulogne on 14 March during 'Rodeo 188' when, in a dogfight, he damaged a Bf 109. During that same engagement the Wing lost four Spitfires – two from No 611 Sqn, one from No 340 Sqn and the aeroplane flown by Wing Leader Wg Cdr 'Dickie' Milne – to JG 26. BS451 served through to the end of the war, and in 1947 it was transferred to the South African Air Force. Colloredo-Mansfeld was killed in action leading Spitfire IX-equipped No 132 Sqn on 7 January 1944.

28
Spitfire VC EE624/TM-R of Sqn Ldr J R C Kilian, No 504 'County of Nottingham' Sqn, Ibsley, 4 April 1943

New Zealander John Kilian had the unusual distinction of commanding four squadrons on operations. He led No 504 Sqn between March and July 1943, flying over western France. He took over EE624 from his predecessor, and was flying it on 4 April when, in a combat in mid-Channel, he damaged an Fw 190 to register his final claim. He flew it regularly throughout the summer, leading a 'Ramrod' in the fighter on 3 May for example. Kilian later flew Corsairs in the Pacific with the RNZAF. Both he and his aircraft survived the war.

29
Spitfire VB AD536/PJ-Z of Lt J Andrieux, No 130 Sqn, Drem and Ballyhalbert, April-May 1943

'Jaco' Andrieux was a pre-war *Armée de l'Air* pilot who fled France to join the RAF, being posted to 130 Sqn as an NCO in September 1941. He registered a number of claims with the unit prior to it moving from the south coast to Scotland and Northern Ireland for a rest. There, during the spring of 1942, Andrieux regularly flew AD536 after it was delivered to the unit from No 602 Sqn at the end of March. He decorated it with a small Free French Air Force marking and his nickname on the port side beneath the cockpit. Andrieux flew this aircraft nine times in April and on most days during May. During its previous service with No 602 Sqn, AD536 had been used by Sqn Ldr Finucane to shoot down 1.5 Fw 190s on 13 March and share in the probable destruction of a Ju 88 the following day.

30
Spitfire IX BS248/AH-O of Capt O Djönne, No 332 (Norwegian) Sqn, North Weald, April-May 1943

BS248 joined No 332 Sqn in October 1942 and served with it for a year, during which time it became an 'ace' aircraft it its own right. On 12 March 1943 Capt Marius Eriksen shot down an Fw 190 with BS248 for his sixth victory. Soon after the fighter was adopted by Olav Djönne as his regular mount, and in it on 13 April he claimed his second victory when, off the Normandy coast, he shot down an Fw 190. Then, during a sortie over the Dutch island of Walcheren on 2 May, he destroyed two more Focke-Wulfs. Finally, on 22 May, over Bruges, Djönne became an ace when he shot down another Fw 190. Both Djönne and BS248 survived the war, with the Spitfire subsequently being transferred to the Royal Danish Air Force.

31
Spitfire IX LZ997/KH-A of Flt Lt W A Conrad, No 403 Sqn RCAF, Lashenden and Headcorn, June-August 1943

Having become an ace over the desert, Canadian Wally Conrad returned to action when he joined No 403 Sqn in England in May 1943 as a flight commander. LZ997 was allocated as his usual mount, and in it he soon began scoring by shooting down an Fw 190 over Belgium on 6 July. Further claims in LZ997 followed until 17 August when, over Bergues on the French coast, he was engaged in a dogfight and shared in the destruction of an Fw 190 with Flt Sgt Graham Shouldice. Moments later the pair collided, and Conrad was forced to bail out and his wingman was killed. The Canadian managed to evade capture and return to action as CO of No 421 Sqn in early 1944.

32
Spitfire IX MH434/ZD-B of Flt Lt H P Lardner-Burke, No 222 Sqn, Hornchurch August-September 1943

South African Pat Lardner-Burke had become a Hurricane ace over Malta in 1941, and in March 1943 he joined No 222 Sqn for operations over France. By August he was using MH434 as his personal aircraft, to which he is understood to have added his wife's name Mylcraine – the aircraft survives today with the Old Flying Machine Company at Duxford and is thus adorned, along with his scoreboard. The latter is shown in the illustration, although it remains to be confirmed that it was indeed carried in 1943. Lardner-Burke's first claim in MH434 came on 27 August when, covering B-17s at 26,000 ft, he dived after nine Fw 190s that had attempted to attack the bombers. Lardner-Burke opened fire and hit one, before going after a second aircraft that he struck with a five-second burst. He watched the latter machine crash near Calais. It was his sixth confirmed victory. Still flying MH434, Lardner-Burke shot down another Focke-Wulf on 5 September and shared in the destruction of a Bf 109G three days later for his final victory.

33
Spitfire VB BM515/VL-P of Flg Off J L Plesman, No 322 (Dutch) Sqn, Llanbedr and Woodvale, August-December 1943

After No 322 Sqn was formed as the first Dutch-manned fighter squadron in June 1943, HRH Prince Bernhard of Lippe-Biesterfeld visited the unit three months later to attend a ceremony at which aircraft were given Dutch names – BM515 became *Princes Beatrix*. They also wore the inverted Dutch triangle marking. Thus adorned, the fighter was flown by the unit on defensive patrols off the coast of northwest England. During this period future V1 ace Flg Off Jan Plesman regularly flew it – he was killed in action in September 1944. BM515 remained with the Dutch squadron until 1944, when it was passed on to a training unit.

34
Spitfire IX BS458/KB of Lt Col K Birksted, No 132 Airfield, North Weald, August-October 1943

Notionally on the strength of No 332 Sqn from October 1942, BS458 was used by No 132 Airfield's Wing Leader, initially Lt Col Helge Mehre, during 1943. The fighter carried his initials HM, and he shot down an Fw 190 over Abbeville in it on 16 July for his final victory. Mehre passed the aircraft on to his successor, Dane Lt Col Kaj Birksted, who shot down a Bf 109 near Dixmuide with it on 14 September for his sixth victory. The aircraft was returned to the manufacturers on 4 October whilst Birksted continued to lead his Wing in another mount. In addition to the pilot's initials and rank pennant, the aircraft also carried the No 64 Sqn scarabee badge and the name *Atchashihar*.

35
Spitfire VB EN950/DN-P of Flt Lt A H Sager, No 416 Sqn RCAF, Digby, 13 November 1943

This aircraft served only briefly with No 416 Sqn, to whom it was delivered on 12 October. Leading an attack on targets in Holland on 13 November, Flt Lt Art Sager was at its controls when the fighter was hit just behind the cockpit by flak on crossing the coast. Sager flew EN950 back to Digby, from where it was sent off for repair. A few weeks later Sager was rested, although he returned to operations with No 416 Sqn in 1944 and claimed two more victories to achieve acedom.

36
Spitfire IX MJ845/HBW of Wg Cdr H A C Bird-Wilson, No 122 Airfield, Harrowbeer, October-December 1943

During late 1943 the Wing Leader of No 122 Airfield was Wg Cdr Harold Bird-Wilson, who adopted MJ845 as his personal mount. In addition to his rank pennant, the aircraft wore his initials and he decorated the rudder with a gauntlet inspired by the badge of No 17 Sqn – the unit he had become an ace with in 1940. When Bird-Wilson left his position at the end of the year MJ845 was handed on to his successor, and fellow ace, Wg Cdr Peter Wickham. Both pilots survived the war, as did their mount, which was scrapped in 1947.

BIBLIOGRAPHY

Bowyer, Michael, *Fighting Colours*. PSL, 1969 and 1975
Caygill, Peter, *Spitfire Mk V in Action*. Airlife, 2001
Cossey, Bob, *Tigers (No 74 Sqn)*. Arms & Armour Press, 1992
Deere, Gp Capt Alan C, *Nine Lives*. Hodder & Stoughton, 1959
Donnet, Lt Gen Michael, *Flight to Freedom*. Wingham Press, 1991
Duke, Sqn Ldr Neville, *War Diaries 1941-1944*, Grub Street, 1995
Duncan-Smith, Gp Capt W G G, *Spitfire into Battle*. John Murray, 1981
Fergusson, Aldon, *Beware, Beware (No 611 Sqn)*. Airfield Publications, 2004
Flintham, Vic and Thomas, Andrew, *Combat Codes*. Airlife, 2003 and 2008
Franks, Norman, *The Greatest Air Battle*. Grub Street, 1992
Griffin John and Kostenuk, Samuel, *RCAF Sqn Histories and Aircraft*. Stevens, 1977
Halley, James, *Squadrons of the RAF and Commonwealth*. Air Britain, 1988
Herrington, John, *Australians in the War 1939-45, Series 3 Volume 3*. Halstead Press, 1962
Houlton, Johnnie, *Spitfire Strikes*. John Murray, 1985
Hovey, H R and Schmidt, D, *416 Squadron History*. Hangar Bookshelf, 1984
Jefford, Wg Cdr C G, *RAF Squadrons*. Airlife 1988 and 2001
Kennedy, Sqn Ldr I F, *Black Crosses off my Wingtip*. General Store, 1994
McIntosh, Dave, *High Blue Battle (No 401 Sqn)*. Spa Books 1990
Matusiak, Wojtek, *Polish Wings, Vols 13, 15 and 16*. Stratus, 2011 and 2012
Mitchell, Alan W, *New Zealanders in the Air War*. Harrap, 1945
Milberry, Larry and Halliday, Hugh, *The RCAF at War 1939-1945* CANAV Books, 1990
Official, *The RCAF Overseas – The First Four Years*. OUP, 1944
Oxspring, Gp Capt Bobby, *Spitfire Command*. William Kimber, 1984
Page, Geoffrey, *Shot Down in Flames*. Grub Street, 1990
Palmer, Derek, *Fighter Squadron (No 19 Sqn)*. Self-Publishing Association, 1991
Rawlings, John D R, *Fighter Squadrons of the RAF*. Macdonald, 1969
Richards, Denis, *RAF Official History 1939-45, Parts 2 and 3*. HMSO, 1954
Robertson, Bruce, *Spitfire – The Story of a Famous Fighter*. Harleyford, 1960
Ross, David et al, *The Greatest Squadron of Them All (No 603 Sqn)*. Grub Street, 2003
Sampson, Wg Cdr R W F and Franks, Norman, *Spitfire Offensive*. Grub Street, 2002
Sands, Flg Off R P D, *Treble One (No 111 Sqn)*. North Weald, 1957
Sarkar, Dilip, *A Few of the Many*. Ramrod, 1995
Shores, Christopher, *Those Other Eagles*. Grub Street, 2004
Shores, Christopher and Williams, Clive, *Aces High, Vols 1 and 2*. Grub Street, 1994 and 1999
Smith, Richard C, *Hornchurch Offensive*. Grub Street, 2001
Smith, Vera, *So Much Sadness, So Much Fun (RAF Ibsley)*. Short Run Books, 2002
Southall, Ivan, *Bluey Truscott*. Angus & Robertson, 1958
Spurdle, Sqn Ldr Bob, *The Blue Arena*. William Kimber, 1985
Sturtivant, Ray et al, *Spitfire International*. Air Britain, 2002
Thomas, Chris and Shores, Christopher, *2nd Tactical Air Force, Vol 1*. Classic, 2005
Tidy, Douglas, *I Fear No Man (No 74 Sqn)*. Macdonald, 1972
Walpole, Gp Capt Nigel, *Dragon Rampant (No 234 Sqn)*. Merlin Massara, 2007
Walsh, Tom, *Remembering the Canadian Yanks*. Publishamerica, 2012
Watkins, David, *Fear Nothing (No 501 Sqn)*. Newton, 1990
Wells, Kevin, *The New Zealand Spitfire Squadron (No 485 Sqn)*. Hutchinson, 1984

INDEX

References to images are in **bold**; references to plate captions are in brackets.

Adolph, Hptm Walter 45
Air Defence of Great Britain (ADGB) 83, 85
aircraft, British: B-17; 64, 65, 67; Blenheim 8, 23; Hurricane 8, 15; Short Stirling 29; *see also* Spitfires
aircraft, German: Bf 109; 8, 11, 13, 17, 20–21, 23, 26, 48; Do 17; 7–8; Do 217; 63, 64; Fw 190; 45, 46, 47, 48, 50, 58–60, 66; He 60; 20; He 111; **17**, 18, 21, 30; He 114; 48; Ju 34; 45; Ju 87; 10; Ju 88; 8, 9, 63; Me 109; 11, 25, 26, 28
Allen, Flt Lt 'Dizzy' 12, 28
Allied Expeditionary Air Force (AEAF) 83, 85
Anderton, Sgt Clive **78**, 79
Archer, Sqn Ldr Philip 25, 58, 77
Armstrong, Sqn Ldr Hugo 'Sinker' 65, 66, **68**, 70
Austeen, Lt Arne 59

Babbage, Plt Off Cyril 45
Bader, Wg Cdr Douglas 20, 26, 31
Balmforth, Sqn Ldr Tommy 59
Balthazar, Hptm Wilhelm 27, 28
Bartley, Flg Off Tony 9
Beamish, Gp Capt Victor 50, 52, 54
Beresford, Sqn Ldr Tristram 'Tommy' 27, 28
Berg, Lt Rolf Arne **61**, 63, 70
Beurling, Flt Lt George 'Screwball' 87
Birksted, Lt Col Kaj 62, **85**, 86
Bisdee, Flg Off John 23, 25
Blake, Sqn Ldr Minden 14, **30**
Blatchford, Wg Cdr 'Cowboy' 72, 74
Blitz, the 14, 16, 18, 21
Bocock, Plt Off Eric 50, 63
Boulding, Flg Off Roger 21–22
Boulter, Flt Lt John 9, 12
Boulton, Sqn l dr Foss 75
Boyd, Wg Cdr Finlay 50, 72
Bradshaw, Flt Lt Anthony 84
Broadhurst, Wg Cdr Harry 13, 24, 26, 28
Brothers, Sqn Ldr Peter 54
Buys, Flt Lt Theo 23, 25

Cameron, Flt Lt Lorne 71, 86
Cameron, Flg Off Neil 49
Casson, Flg Off 'Buck' 20, 31, **32**
Chadburn, Sqn Ldr Lloyd 53, 74, **76**, 77, 81, 82
Charles, Flg Off 'Jack' 18–19, 24, 30, 75–76, 79
Checketts, Sqn Ldr Johnny **72**, 76, 79
Chisholm, Sgt Keith 45–46
Christie, Flt Lt Pat 7
Churchill, Winston 24
Conrad, Flt Lt Wally 78
Cox, Sgt David 26–27
Crawford-Compton, Flt Lt Bill 54, 64, 71
Crowley-Milling, Flt Lt Denis 24, 32, 62
Currant, Sqn Ldr 'Bunny' 46, 57

Darling, Plt Off 'Mitzi' **17**, 56
De Courcey, Sgt Tommy 64
Deere, Sqn Ldr Al 18, 56, 70–71, 72, 75
Demozay, Flt Lt Jean-François 'Moses' 48, **49**, 65–66
Dexter, Flg Off Peter 30, 31
Dieppe 60–65
Dodd, Flt Lt Wilbert 82
Donnet, Plt Off Michel 59
Du Monceau de Bergendael, Plt Off Yvan 32, 52–53, 56, 62, 82
Duke, Plt Off Neville 19, 26, 31
Duke-Woolley, Sqn Ldr Myles 47, 50, 56, 61
Duncan-Smith, Plt Off Wilf 11, 23–24, 30, 45, 54, 56, 59
Dundas, Flg Off 'Cocky' 8, 20, 31

Duperier, Cdt Bernard 66
Durnford, Sgt Peter 51, 63, 67

Edsall, Flg Off Eric 48
Ehlers, Obfw Hans 74
Eriksen, Sgt Marius 59–60, 61, 70, 74
Exercise *Spartan* 71, 78
Eyre, Wg Cdr Tony 52

Faber, Oblt Armin 57–58
Farquhar, Wg Cdr Andrew 22
Fearnley, Lt Fredrik 57, 86
Finlay, Wg Cdr Don 59
Finucane, Wg Cdr Brendan 'Paddy' 6, 7, 8–9, 11, 30, 46, 52, 53, 57, 58
Fokes, Flt Lt Ronnie **6**, 10, 19
Freeborn, Sqn Ldr Johnny 76

Galland, Oblt Adolf 17, 18, 24, 46, 49
Gardner, Flt Lt Peter 30–31
Gaze, Flt Lt Tony 29, 58–59, 80
Gibbs, Wg Cdr Pat 63–64
Godefroy, Flg Off Hugh 69, 71, 77, 78
Gouby, Adj Robert 66, **68**, 70
Grant, Sgt Reg 24, 51
Gribble, Flt Lt George 22–23

Harries, Sqn Ldr Ray 53, 70
Heglund, Capt Svein 63, 70, 79–80, 81
Hesselyn, Flg Off Ray 80, 81–82
Hilken, Sgt Clive 27
Holden, Sqn Ldr Ken 29
Houlton, Plt Off Johnnie 81
Howard-Williams, Flg Off Peter 32, 71–72
Howell, Sqn Ldr Frank 19, 30
Hughes-Rees, Sgt David 30
Hugo, Sqn Ldr 'Dutch' 52, 55, 61
Hull, Plt Off Johnnie 63, 67
Hulse, Sgt Graham 'Ginger' 65
Humphrey, Plt Off Andrew 21, 31

Jameson, Sqn Ldr 'Jamie' 14, 18, 21, 27, 70
Johnson, Sgt Bill 10, 26
Johnson, Sqn Ldr 'Johnnie' 8, 15, 31, 62, 64, 72–73, 75
Johnstone, Sqn Ldr 'Tim' 87

Kayll, Wg Cdr Joe 26
Kilburn, Flt Lt Mike 63, **65**, 67
Kingaby, Sqn Ldr Don 25, 28, 59, 70, 71
Kingcome, Sqn Ldr Brian 50, 56

Lacey, Flt Lt 'Ginger' 30
Lambert, Sqn Ldr Jim 86
Lardner-Burke, Flt Lt Pat 80
Lawson, Flt Lt Walter 26, 32
Lefevre, Sqn Ldr 'Pip' 73
Leigh Malory, ACM Sir Trafford 83
Levesque, Sgt Omer 47, 50
Lock, Flt Lt Eric 29, 31
Lofts, Sqn Ldr Keith 82
Lovell, Flt Lt Tony 16, **17**, 46–47

MacDonald, Flg Off Harry 71, 76, 85
Mackie, Plt Off Evan 54, **55**
McNair, Plt Off 'Buck' 46, 77, 78
Magwood, Plt Off Charles 52, 73, 75
Malan, Wg Cdr A G 'Sailor' 10, **15**, 24, 28, 75
Mann, Sgt Jackie 17
Marples, Flt Lt Roy 45
Marrs, Plt Off Eric 'Boy' 7–8, 31
Mehre, Maj Helge 61–62, 78
Milne, Wg Cdr 'Dickie' **68**, 69–70
Mohr, Maj Wilhelm 61
Mölders, Oblt Werner 11, 13, 14, 20
Moore, Plt Off Leslie 80–81, 82

Morrison, Sgt Don 47, 50, 53, 62, 67
Mortimer-Rose, Flt Lt Edward 14
Mottram, Flt Lt Roy 26, 32
Mouchotte, Cdr Rene 75–76, 80
Moynet, Sous Lt André 67
Mrazek, Sqn Ldr Karel 55
Mungo-Park, Sqn Ldr John 22, 23, 27

Newbery, Flt Lt Dickie 72, 79
Newling, Flt Lt Mike 14
Northcott, Sqn Ldr Geoff **76**, 77
Nowell, WO Garry 72, 77

Oeseau, Hptm Walter 11
Offenberg, Flg Off Jean 19, 25
Ogilvie, Flg Off Keith 23, 28–29
Operations 24, 49–52, 58, 60–65
Oxspring, Sqn Ldr Bobby 49–50, 56–57

Parker, Sqn Ldr Tom 61
Pavey, Flg Off Alan 82
Payne, Sgt William 10, 23
Powell, Wg Cdr Peter 56
Prihoda, Plt Off Josef 51, 57
Priller, Hptm 'Pips' 46, 56

Rae, Flt Sgt Jack 50–51, 75
Rankin, Sqn Ldr Jamie 12, 15, 19, 23, 56–57, 79
Ratten, Wg Cdr John 76–77
Reilhac, Lt Eugene **68**, 69
Rigler, Sgt Tommy 20–21, 25, 49
Robillard, Sgt Larry 28
Robinson, Wg Cdr Michael 54
Royal Air Force (RAF) 6–7, 52
Royal Australian Air Force (RAAF) 30, 66
Royal Canadian Air Force (RCAF) 46, 47, 52, 53, 62, 70
Royal Navy 9, 52
Royal Norwegian Air Force 61–62
Ryder, Wg Cdr Norman 46

Sager, Flt Off Art 80, 84
Saunders, Plt Off Cecil **6**, 10
Scott-Malden, Flt Lt David 22, 32, **52**, 56, 57, 61
Sheen, Flt Lt Des 14, 30
Shepherd, Flt Lt John 64, 78–79
Sheppard, Flt Lt Jack 84–85
Sognnes, Lt Helge 74, 77
Spitfires 8, **33–44** (90–95); I 9, **19**; II 12, 14, **20**; V 9–10, 14, 15, 22, 73–74; VI 55, **67**; VII 72; IX 58, 59, 60, **69**, 74, 83, 85; VB **46**, 48, **53**
Spurdle, Plt Off Bob 'Spud' 13–14, 16, 17–18
Stapleton, Sqn Ldr Frederick 'Eric' 20, 22, 23, 31
Stenborg, Plt Off Gray 55

Tactical Air Forces (TAFs) 71, 76, 83, 85
Thomas, Wg Cdr Eric 65
Thorold-Smith, Flg Off 'Throttle' 46
Tradin, Lt Rolf 76
Truscott, Plt Off 'Bluey' 45–46, 50, 53
Tuck, Wg Cdr Bob Stanford 49

US Air Force (USAF) 60, 68, 70, 83, 85

Van Mentz, Flt Lt Brian 14, 19
Vasatko, Wg Cdr Alois 55, 57

Watkins, Flt Lt Douglas 'Dirty' 13, 61
Webb, Sqn Ldr Paul 49
Wells, Flt Lt 'Hawkeye' 29, 51
Wickham, Sqn Ldr Peter 60
Willis, Flg Off Oliver 76
Wing Leaders 14–15, **21**
Wipiti, WO Bert 81
Woodhouse, Sqn Ldr H de C A 'Paddy' 19
Wootton, Plt Off 'Bertie' 14, 74